The Women's Guide to Successful Investing

Achieving Financial Security and Realizing Your Goals

Nancy Tengler

First published in 2014 by
PALGRAVE MACMILLAN®
in the United States—a division of St. Martin's Press LLC,
175 Fifth Avenue, New York, NY 10010.

Where this book is distributed in the UK, Europe and the rest of the world,
this is by Palgrave Macmillan, a division of Macmillan Publishers Limited,
registered in England, company number 785998, of Houndmills,
Basingstoke, Hampshire RG21 6XS.

Palgrave Macmillan is the global academic imprint of the above companies
and has companies and representatives throughout the world.

Palgrave® and Macmillan® are registered trademarks in the United States,
the United Kingdom, Europe and other countries.

ISBN: 978–1–137–40334–6

Library of Congress Cataloging-in-Publication Data

Tengler, Nancy.
    The women's guide to successful investing : achieving financial security
and realizing your goals / Nancy Tengler.
        pages cm
    ISBN 978–1–137–40334–6 (hardback)
        1. Women—Finance, Personal. 2. Investments. 3. Stocks—Prices.
    I. Title.

HG179.T4196 2014
332.6082—dc23   2014005402

A catalogue record of the book is available from the British Library.

Design by Newgen Knowledge Works (P) Ltd., Chennai, India.

First edition: August 2014

10 9 8 7 6 5 4 3 2 1

CONTENTS

ILLUSTRATIONS

FIGURES

TABLES

FOREWORD

I grew up not really thinking about money, or the role money plays in our life. My childhood was spent in a small town in Canada, where both my parents worked full time to be able to provide for me and my sister. We certainly had enough but there was never talk of the stock market, or interest rates, or an investment philosophy. It was more of a money in and money out lifestyle, which is the way most people I knew seemed to live. It was not until I went off to college and decided upon a career in finance that the world of money and markets opened up to me, and there was no going back. Upon graduation I went to work at Goldman Sachs in New York City and in 1996 became the youngest woman and first female trader to become a partner of the firm. I was in the business of helping clients make money on their financial assets and I grew to understand the role the capital markets played in our economy and our world. I also grew to understand how at the individual level learning at least the basics around saving, investing, and budgeting were core life skills that everyone should possess. Money is not an ends, it is a means to an ends. By learning about how to manage your financial assets you are resourcing your dreams, your passions, and your future. The core knowledge contained in this book is sadly not knowledge we likely have got through standard education. We have to choose to learn it. We have to opt in. So congratulations on embracing the journey to become financially literate and financially empowered. As women we owe it to ourselves to embrace the power that is in our pocketbooks, in our bank accounts, and in our investment portfolios to not only provide for our own future and that of our family, but to help shape the world we want to live in.

JACKI ZEHNER—CEO, Women Moving Millions

PREFACE

It's Time to Raise Our Financial IQ

A very long time ago, when I began working in the investment business, the activity was housed in the trust department of large banks. Our clients were the heirs of wealth most often accumulated by someone else. Generally they were placid and uninterested in the investment process and had only one single overriding concern: receiving their monthly distribution check. Rarely did we meet with clients, though we were responsible for the day-to-day management of their money. Investing, to borrow from an old quote, was like making sausage—our clients seemed to think it best not to see how it was being done. So, of course, meeting with our largest client stands out starkly. Mrs. H was a regal but spunky widow. She dressed impeccably down to her matching hat and gloves and carried herself with the air of a woman of the world. Mrs. H understood the power and importance of investing. She was interested in every detail we discussed about her portfolios. Most remarkable, she understood the importance of taking *enough* risk. Why did we need to own so many bonds, she wanted to know? Why not more stocks? And though the first rule every investor learns is to diversify in order to spread risk, I had to agree her question had merit. Why didn't we own a greater percentage in stocks? They consistently outperformed the bond portion of her portfolios and she hardly needed the income the bonds produced.

Mrs. H was a wonderful role model for women investors: generous, kind, adventuresome, and prudent. Prudent because she informed herself and in doing so understood the important role risk played in her investment portfolios. As a client, she was also extraordinarily rare. Few of my subsequent women clients understood the importance of taking a part in the management of their wealth. Much later in my career I resigned from managing the account of a wealthy young woman who was so dangerously uninterested in how we were investing her funds (though she was entirely dependent upon the money) I simply didn't want her as a client. I had learned that those clients unwilling to learn the basics were ultimately the worst—their instincts were entirely driven by emotion and therefore dangerous to their own wealth.

Academics Annamaria Lusardi and Olivia S. Mitchell published a paper in 2006 on financial literacy.[1] Their findings, while startling, line up with my twenty-plus years of managing billions of dollars of other people's money. Most people don't understand the most basic economic and investing concepts nor are they particularly interested in mastering them. In their review of the available research, Lusardi and Mitchell found that on a basic test administered by the National Council on Economic Education, American adults earned, on average, a C grade while high-school students flunked entirely. As women we have a significant reason to learn about finance and investing: we tend to live longer. And because we tend to live longer, we will at some point be responsible for the financial management of our assets. And presumably because of our longevity we will also need more money than our male counterparts for retirement.

Two professors at Colorado State University, Vickie L. Bajtelsmit and Alexandra Bernasek, published an academic paper exploring the difference between the way women and men invest.[2] The variance is primarily centered around a woman's willingness to take risk. Taking a conservative approach is definitely an advantage when investing but avoiding risk altogether is not. Risk is inherent in every aspect of our lives but it seems more prominent and somehow more dangerous when we invest. Perhaps that is because we measure our results every single day. But the fact is that over the long-term investing is not the risky activity. It's the not investing that contains the most risk to our future security.

Join me in this adventure and you will increase your financial IQ. In doing so you will begin to take control of your own financial future, creating wealth for you and your family. I know your plate is full with the daily business of living and that adding another "to do" seems impossible. But, ladies, our greatest strength is our strength; our ability to squeeze just one more thing into our day and to do it well. With intelligence, grace, and determination. As the former governor of the Great State of Texas Ann Richards once said, "After all, Ginger Rogers did everything that Fred Astaire did. She just did it backwards and in high heels."

NANCY TENGLER
Paradise Valley, Arizona
May 2014

ACKNOWLEDGMENTS

If central casting were to select someone to portray the consummate literary agent he would look and act like Sam Fleishman of Literary Artists Representatives. Sam was a gift to me during every stage of this process. His willingness to encourage and suggest and dig in with both hands is rare and deeply valued. Without his insight and guidance I would still be searching for a direction. He also identified an outstanding publisher in Laurie Harting, Executive Editor of Palgrave Macmillan. Laurie embraced the vision for this book and focused me in ways I likely would have missed without her guidance. Her enthusiasm is something authors dream of; her vast experience and penetrating suggestions produced a much stronger and more relevant book. I am in Sam's and Laurie's debt.

Jacki Zehner, CEO of Women Moving Millions and an astute and successful investor, graciously agreed to write the foreword. Her tireless work for the advancement of women and girls is admirable and worthy. The world is a better place for her passion and kindness. I am humbled that amidst her demanding schedule she found the time to pen the inspirational foreword.

Thanks also to Lauren LoPinto of Palgrave Macmillan for talking me off the technological ledge in the final days of completing this book. Finally, to my husband, Doug, and my children, Chip and M.K., who have lived the principles outlined in this book: thank you. Through innumerable dinner discussions and shopping trips where I checked the shelves and grilled the salespeople or critiqued the service, they have remained patient and bemused. And supportive always.

CHAPTER 1

Wealth Accumulation Is an Attitude: Investing for Your Future Requires a Few Goals and Much Less Capital Than You Think

This book is for women.

Which is not to say it is not for men. Anyone interested in achieving financial independence for themselves and their family will benefit from reading these pages. But, my focus is women—in particular, women who, for too long, have been left out of the financial dialogue. Or have, perhaps, excused themselves from the conversation altogether. Since many women oversee their family finances, this deficit in our financial education creates at best a lost opportunity for the balance sheets of a majority of American households. And because the research shows that at some point in her life virtually every woman will become responsible for managing her family's wealth we owe it to ourselves to become more financially savvy. Yet, most of us feel largely unprepared for the task. Three-quarters of women interviewed—no matter their level of education—told researchers they wished they had learned more about financial matters. And they confess to sending their children out largely unprepared as well.

Financial independence is achieved through two distinct disciplines: saving and investing. Equally as important and equally elusive, both are necessary ingredients to expand wealth. And that is our objective: to maximize wealth accumulation so you are able to reach your individual and family's long-term objectives. To that end we will endeavor together to raise your saving and investing awareness. We will develop an understanding of how to successfully invest in the stock and bond markets through the identification and implementation of eleven Intelligent Investing Rules that will increase confidence in buying and selling stocks. In the end we will inevitably raise our financial IQ and, therefore, our likelihood of achieving financial independence.

Cultivate the Habit of Saving

Most of us—whether we engage in the practice or not—understand very clearly *how* to save money. Whether we do so or not is a matter of discipline or, in some cases, a lack of income. The vast majority of Americans are capable of saving. They simply lack the discipline. For many years my lack of saving discipline placed me at the head of that undisciplined mass of spenders. Having grown up in a home where my single mom worked two jobs, I learned to work, scrimp, and save from a very early age. By the time I hit my late twenties, I was ready to spend. Then the children came and the myriad expenses of growing them up: soccer cleats, baseball gloves, swim goggles, golf clubs, piano lessons, more swim goggles, and then one day: college. Spending had become a habit; any instinct I once had for saving was long ago repressed by the habit (and enjoyment) of spending. I had saving amnesia and, worse, I found myself making excuses about why I didn't save. What was the point of stashing a few hundred dollars each month? I convinced myself it would make no difference.

Then, at some point, I rediscovered the literary classic *A Tree Grows in Brooklyn*. Francie Nolan's dirt-poor, immigrant grandmother provided a lesson in saving that shamed me back into the game. She counseled Francie's mother to save whatever she could manage—even pennies each day, "The money will grow." Soon, "there will be a small fortune." The practice of saving begets more saving, becomes a habit, and eventually we find ourselves looking for opportunities not to spend when spending isn't necessary. I am not offering a draconian alternative to living but rather an attitude that balances the opportunity to set aside a little something for the future against the desire to consume today.

The study of behavioral economics explores the psychological challenges individuals face when it comes to saving. Numerous studies have been conducted and numerous papers written to explain the problem that many of us have with saving money for our futures. One of the most vocal and prolific researchers in behavioral finance is Dr. Shlomo Benartzi, professor of UCLA Anderson School of Management and chief behavioral economist for Allianz Global Investors Center for Behavioral Finance. His work shows that "only 1 out of 10 Americans are saving enough for their retirement."[1] Dr. Benartzi concludes that one of the three main factors that prevent us from saving is immediate gratification—the desire to spend today. He is right, of course. Many of us spend today because we spend too little time considering future needs. Add to that the magnitude of saving often required to meet future goals is so great we simply choose to ignore the problem. Many years ago when I was juggling family and career a colleague of mine suggested I find ways to solve my logistical problems with money. His argument was that I had more money than time. That is not to say I had an abundance of money but I had almost no free time. Hiring someone to help with house cleaning or yard work released me from the frenetic pace I was keeping and gave me more time with my family. Of course, there will always be times when spending will be the right solution. But had I retained saving as a habit I would have found ways to spend less, to avoid opportunities to spend unnecessarily. If my attitude had been one of saving a predetermined amount I might have then supplemented my penchant for consumer brands with generics. I would have pumped my own gas instead of driving through the full-service lane or had my children clean the house and mow the lawns (as they eventually did) rather than pay to do so. Rooting out wasteful spending—which I did in the office—would have saved hundreds, perhaps thousands, of dollars each month, money I could have tucked away for future investment. Ultimately, after Francie Nolan's grandmother gave me a figurative slap up side the head—I did just that.

Soon I had set aside enough money to invest for a series of goals our family had established.

SAVING, EVEN A LITTLE, MATTERS

If you are like me (and apparently 90 percent of other Americans) you spend more than you need to. As an intelligent woman you don't need me to advise you on debt management or how to construct a monthly budget, rather I am simply reminding you of the need to save. And the need to save as much as you possibly can. One of the most common fallacies I encounter comes from women who believe it is too late to save and invest. Whatever your age or stage in life you still have time to save and work toward financial independence.

According to a 2010 study conducted by the Boston Consulting Group titled "Leveling the Playing Field," women tend to be long-term in focus, and very concerned about potential life-stage events (like sending their children to college or saving for their own retirement) that will affect their investment needs.[2] Our priorities and goals are clear: We want to provide for our families' future financial needs. And the only way to do that is to save. Let's look at a few examples to provide some perspective and increase our saving IQ.

Woman #1: 35 years old, two children, married, stay-at-home mom. Expectations are that both children will attend a four-year college. Husband plans to retire in 25 years. Finances are tight but Woman #1 is able to tuck away $100 per month. Because like 70 percent of women, she does not consider herself an investor but a saver, she places her savings in a money market account. Since rates fluctuate and are more likely to rise than decline from this point we are going to calculate her return based on an interest rate of 2.5 percent (money market rates are currently a little less than 0.5 percent but expectations are that rates will continue to rise over the next few years so we will assume 2.5 percent): **$41,618.**

Woman #2: 45 years old, no children, unmarried. She plans to retire at 60 to engage in volunteer work. Currently she is tucking away $500 per month and, again, like 70 percent of women, she does not consider herself an investor. She is a saver. So her savings also go into an interest-bearing account at her bank. In fifteen years, assuming a 2.5 percent interest rate, she will have amassed **$109,062.**

Woman #3: 55 years old, adult children, married, and both their spouses are working. She plans to retire (as does her husband) in five years. She and her husband are saving $1,000 per month and believe that because they are close to retirement they should park their money in a savings account. At our assumed rate of 2.5 percent the couple will have accumulated **$63,481.**

Saving, even a little, does matter.

Spending Is the Anti-saving

As a professional investor, college professor, and mother I appreciate the importance of repetition when I am interested in driving home a point. So allow me to share with you a spending experience that has haunted me for over twenty-five years. In September 1988, two weeks after my first child was born, I engaged in two major transactions in one week: a purchase and an investment. We will discuss the investment in a moment but for now we are concerned with the purchase.

I was scheduled to make a presentation to a new, $100 million client. None of my business suits fit and I was not going to be caught dead in a maternity outfit after the fact—especially the maternity clothes available to working women in the late 1980s (but that is a story for a different book). I gathered up my new baby, stroller, diaper bag, blankets, and pacifier—the whole chaotic collection—and rushed to the mall. I bought almost the first thing I found: a knee-length sweater that draped discreetly over the extra pounds and looked surprisingly professional. When the clerk commented on the soft cashmere material, no bells went off. I didn't live in a cashmere world, had never worn cashmere, and clearly had no idea of the expense or the impracticality. All I cared about was that it fit. Cradling my now restless baby in one arm, diaper bag slung over one shoulder, my purse over the other, I signed the receipt without examining it, dashed back home, and packed for my flight later that evening. Consumed with home life, I didn't give the sweater another thought. Dressing for the meeting the following afternoon, I removed the tag and saw the price for the first time: $1,099. One thousand ninety-nine dollars! Plus tax. Due at my client's in 15 minutes with nothing else to wear and despite the overwhelming, choking realization of my stunning stupidity I now owned that reckless decision.

Twenty-five years later the sweater still hangs in my closet. It is wrinkled and bally as only cashmere can be and sports a few moth holes. That conspicuous purchase is a reminder of a time when spending rather than saving became a potentially ruinous habit.

Buying a $1,099 sweater—as outrageous as it was—represented only part of the expense equation; it is important to understand that there was a real cost and also an *opportunity cost* of my perilous sweater purchase. To calculate the real, out-of-pocket expense of that poor choice I would have to consider the dollar amount spent ($1,099), plus tax of approximately $80 and credit card interest of close to $220—I didn't have the heart nor the means to pay it off at once. Perhaps the most important cost, however, was the **opportunity cost**. Think of opportunity cost in dating parlance as the one who got away. It is the cost of not doing something or at the very least not doing the right thing. In addition to the actual cost of the sweater, the opportunity cost of my decision to purchase the sweater was the foregone accumulation and compounding of interest had I saved the money, or the appreciation potentially earned if I had taken the sweater money and invested it in my second transaction that week—a stock (discussed below). The real and opportunity cost of that foolish and impulsive purchase still echoes.

SAVING TO INVEST IS THE WISEST STRATEGY

The second element required to achieve financial independence involves investing. As soon I say, "Nobody gets rich saving—you must invest," I will receive hundreds of emails disputing my claim and describing Great Aunt Edith who lived in the family home with her cats, took in sewing, and left her nieces and nephews $1 million upon her death at the ripe old age of 98 years. Let's stipulate for purposes of my illustration that some people really can become wealthy by saving alone—if they live long enough. The vast majority, however, become wealthy or retire comfortably or put their five children through college debt-free by a combination of the two activities: saving and investing.

Investing is not gambling. Nor is it a scientific mystery inaccessible to average individuals. Investing is a long-term discipline that will generate excellent returns for patient investors. It is no coincidence that all of the great investors, those celebrated by the financial media and professionals, are long-term, disciplined investors who establish and stick with their investing discipline in good markets and bad. My objective is to aid you in determining how to establish an appropriate discipline that you will feel comfortable employing during good markets and difficult markets. Markets like the financial crisis in 2008–2009.

To illustrate the value of long-term investing let's consider my second transaction during that fateful week twenty-five years ago.

In a largely symbolic gesture, I purchased one share of IBM stock for our son. I thought it would be fun to hang the certificate on his wall and use it as an object lesson to teach him about things financial. Before I could get the share framed, I misplaced it and so the lesson was, for the most part, lost. But because I lost the share, I forgot all about it and consequently left the investment (correctly) alone. Each quarter for the next twenty-five years the dividend paid by the company was reinvested in an incremental share of IBM stock. That approximately $100 investment returned 1,020 percent or 10.6 percent per year through the end of September 2013. During that period there have been two colossally devastating **bear markets** that frightened investors mistakenly into cash all the while our little share of IBM plumped and expanded like bread dough. Though market corrections punched down the dough a few times, fueled by the yeast of earnings (which produce stock price growth and dividend payments) our $100 value has grown at a pace far exceeding the rate of inflation and the return on savings or money market accounts. (For all of you stock market skeptics, it is also important to note that the return on the S&P 500 over that same period was a respectable 797 percent or 9.9 percent per year. Simply investing in the stock market index produced enviable returns as well.)

I chose the time period featured below because it represents my actual experience. But, the passage of time is essential to investing; even if your timing is not perfect and you purchase shares before a market correction or a prolonged period of unimpressive returns (as I unwittingly did: IBM traded sideways, providing almost no appreciation for the first ten years), you will be asking yourself only one question: Why didn't I buy more? That $100 share of IBM is worth over $1,300 because of the reinvestment of dividends and **capital appreciation** of the stock over the holding period. Had I contributed $100 per month to my IBM holdings, and assuming our annualized return over the 25-year period of 10.6 percent, my investment would be worth just shy of $150,000. The powerful combination of saving *and* investing is undeniable.

So, there are two important facts to consider when we make financial decisions. The first is that there is an opportunity cost to spending. Think of spending as the anti-saving. Had I invested that $1,099 in, say, IBM stock as I did for my son, my investment would be worth $11,430 twenty-five years later. Instead of a ragged and useless old sweater I would have a nice little nest egg set aside. My opportunity cost is the $11,430 I didn't earn because I didn't save and invest that money. The second factor is that while saving alone is immensely better than not saving at all, saving and investing are far superior. Had I simply saved the $100 instead of investing it in IBM stock, that $100 would be worth far less than the approximately $1,300 I have earned from my one share purchase. And had I added to that investment $100 each month over the same twenty-five year period my investment would be valued at an approximately eye-popping $150,000.

One more thing about investing in stocks. I understand that the market melt-down of 2008 has placed a number of would-be investors on the sidelines. I understand that our aversion to loss can overpower our desire for return. Market routs like 2008 when stocks in the **S&P 500** plunged 37 percent are the reason many people feel investing *is* like gambling. The losses investors experienced in their portfolios were real and devastating and, to many, excessively arbitrary. For some they were much more than paper losses if the money was needed and stocks had to be sold at the bottom. Others simply lost their nerve and sold into the weakness and the breakneck speed of the stock market's decline wiped out years, even decades, of savings in a matter of months. Worse, in the midst of the crisis the most vocal pundits were telling us that our financial system was broken and had fundamentally changed, adding fuel to the selling blaze. It is easy to see why many investors have stayed on the sidelines over the last five years while the market has about doubled, regaining and surpassing 2008 levels. If we save to provide for our future—a safer future—investing in the stock market can feel a bit too much like spinning a roulette wheel. Is it possible to invest despite the unsettling fear that grips us during declines? Can we develop the discipline to continue investing during markets like 2008—often a once-in-a-lifetime opportunity to buy great companies on sale—while suppressing the urge to bail out? To learn not to zig when we should zag?

Establishing an Investment Discipline That Meets Your Risk Tolerance Is Critical

This will be our challenge: To develop an investment discipline that ensures you will generate long-term capital appreciation and that through practice you will develop the investing muscle memory to follow your discipline even when it is hard to do. We will endeavor to develop a base of knowledge (not technical mumbo jumbo) that will provide the courage to follow your plan despite the dissonance of cyclical economic and market trends. By the time you finish this book you will understand your risk tolerance and you will have developed an investing discipline that suits your goals and those you have established for your family. You will, in short, know exactly where you are going and how to get there. We will establish eleven Intelligent Investing Rules that will guide your actions and reinforce your decisions during good markets and bad.

Intelligent Investing Rule #1: *Having any investment discipline is better than having no discipline at all; once your investment* *strategy is established, never deviate. (But, if you do fall off the wagon, don't give up, get right back on and stay the course.)*

An Example of Staying the Course

When the pundits tell you it is different this time. Remember that there is one tried and true investing tenet: Things are rarely different. It is accurate, however, that companies and their products cycle in and out of favor. It is also true that some formerly very good companies have mismanaged their way out of business: Polaroid and Eastman Kodak come to mind. But the majority of the time, good companies—and especially great companies—stumble, get back on their feet, regroup, and power forward. We are interested in buying great companies managed by great management teams, with the talent and financial wherewithal to overcome any inevitable problems. Starbucks (**stock ticker:** SBUX) is one such company and a growth stock that stumbled dramatically after too rapid growth leading into the financial crisis of 2008. And a company I bought too soon. Buying early is one of the occupational hazards of being an investor. When a growth company disappoints investors, the sentiment quickly changes from love (price appreciation) to hate (price depreciation) to indifference (price stagnation and potential further depreciation). For our purposes we will call these great growth companies that have fallen out of favor **Fallen Angel growth stocks**.

It is important to remember that growth investors can sell out of a holding much faster than value hunters will buy in. In fact, because growth investors are often **momentum** driven they may exit an entire position in a stock if they so much as sniff trouble. When the earnings miss or a new product or distribution glitch manifests they run—don't walk—for the exits. At the same sign of trouble that causes growth investors to flee and the stock price to collapse, the value crowd begins to look more closely at whether or not to buy. It takes time to gather data and analyze the company's business. Time to decide whether or not and when to buy. The intelligent investor's dilemma is to determine when to get into the stock of a great company that has stumbled. Sometimes we are too eager.

When I saw a chance to buy Starbucks in April 2007, I did. The stock had declined 30 percent from a recent high of $40. The company had expanded too quickly; same store sales were declining as new stores cannibalized sales from established locations. I waited for the stock price to stabilize around the $31 level and began to accumulate my holdings. In December 2007, celebrated CEO Howard Schultz returned to the company, and the market cheered Schultz's reengagement with a rally in SBUX stock price. Then the financial crisis of 2008 hit and the market sunk like a stone, dragging Starbucks with it until the stock finally hit bottom under $10 per share. An unmitigated disaster, you might think.

Normally my investing discipline would lead me to buy more of the stock in a great company like Starbucks as it declined but I was busy with grad school and two high-school age kids and I, frankly, wasn't paying close attention to my investments. I did nothing but ride the stock down from $31 to a low of around $8 per share. But here is the compelling fact about buying great companies. You don't have to know the exact day the stock hits bottom. You don't have to be right about every detail. You just have to stick to your discipline and let the company management do the heavy lifting.

Though I bought SBUX far from where it ultimately bottomed, I still generated a return of 15.64 percent per year since my April 27, 2007 purchase, well in excess of the S&P 500's return of 5.47 percent over the same period. Had I bottom-picked the stock toward the end of 2008, I would have received an annual return of (gulp) 61.4 percent versus 21.9 percent for the market. A far superior return, indeed. But getting it mostly right and generating a steady return over time is our objective and despite being too early I did just that. The point is that stock investing is about generating consistent, excess returns over time, not necessarily about securing cocktail party bragging rights. Remember Intelligent Investing Rule #1: Having any investment discipline is better than having no discipline at all; once your investment strategy is established, never deviate. Your allocation to stocks might change as you grow older or grow closer to reaching a particular goal but *how* you buy and sell stocks—your investment discipline or strategy—should not be altered.

How Much Do I Need to Save in Order to Invest?

Investing requires much less capital than most people imagine. Two thousand dollars is a good start. We can make do with even less. But, if you follow a savings pattern similar to the ones described above and invest in stocks you will generate even more wealth on your road to financial independence. If, for example, assuming the long-term average annual return for the stock market over the last 100 years of 9 percent, we can recalculate the three Woman Investor scenarios discussed earlier in the chapter. Following the same patterns of saving outlined previously, Woman #1 ends up with **$112,953** if she invests in stocks versus $41,618 at the end of twenty-five years if she places the money in an interest-bearing bank account. She saves the same $100 per month but the power of subsequently investing the money in stocks results in a far more robust return. The same applies for Woman #2 who now ends up with **$190,621** after fifteen years of investing $500 per month versus $109,062 if she simply saves the same amount. And Woman #3 generates wealth of **$75,989** after five years of investing vs. $63,481 saving $1,000 per month and depositing it in the bank. The takeaway? Investing generates significantly superior returns over saving. And, again, we note that the length of time invested clearly improves total return, but the critical component in achieving higher returns is investing our savings rather than just tucking those savings in the bank at rates that barely (if at all) keep up with inflation. Wealth generation is achieved through investing what we've saved, not simply saving alone.

No matter your age or income, my goal is to raise your financial IQ. To increase your awareness of saving and establish a habit of saving for future life-stage events. To remove the fear and confusion you may have developed toward investing by teaching you how to identify great companies. That knowledge will build your confidence to buy those great companies when their stocks are cheap—companies you will want to own for a lifetime. I can't guarantee you'll always make perfect investments—I don't know any investor who gets it right every time—but I can guarantee that as you build and diversify your holdings you will generate returns over the long-term that will exceed today's money market and certificate of deposit rates and ensure the value of your investments exceed the growth of inflation. And because you will be following a well-defined discipline—think: work-out regimen or diet—even if you make the occasional mistake your effort will produce sound results overall and you will avoid avoid the pitfall of falling financially behind. You will be well on your way to financial independence.

So let's dig in and endeavor to raise our financial and investing IQ.

CHAPTER 2

Why Women Make Excellent Investors: Women Inherently Display the Traits Required for Successful Investing

Let's begin with what the research tells us about women and investing.

Dozens of studies have been conducted over the last two decades examining women's attitudes toward their finances and the topic of investing. Two consistent themes emerge when it comes to individual women investors. First: all the studies conclude that women's portfolios outperform their male counterparts over every time period measured. In up markets and down markets. Every study measuring performance comes to the same conclusion: women are not only excellent investors, but also better than their male counterparts when it come to producing returns. The second recurring conclusion: the reason women seem to consistently produce better investment results is because of attributes inherent to most women. Female investors tend to lack the overconfidence exhibited by most men when it comes to financial matters. From study to study women are consistently identified as more risk averse, willing to acknowledge and research what they don't know, and more deliberate in their trading activity. Each of these traits is correspondingly attributed to outperformance. And each of these traits usually results in reduced levels of risk. The overwhelming conclusion? Women generate better investment performance and lower risk. Naturally.

But the problem is that the vast majority of *women* don't seem to understand their potential strength as investors. Consistent with numerous recent studies, the 2012–2013 Prudential research survey

"Financial Experience & Behaviors Among Women" reveals that they are still, for the most part, not confident in making financial decisions.[1] As we said before, while over 70 percent characterized themselves as "savers," a significant portion still self-identify as lacking financial knowledge and almost two-thirds confirm they are "only interested in guaranteed FDIC-insured products." Women continue to feel comfortable saving but despite what the research shows regarding their ability to generate superior investment performance, they still do not feel they have the knowledge nor the skill base to invest. And their reluctance to do so may have something to do with their attitudes toward investing. The Prudential study cites a new statistic that shows that less than 25 percent of the women interviewed claim to enjoy the "sport" of investing. This characterization is somewhat troubling and may lend insight into why women still shy away from the stock market. Investing is not sport. It is not a game; rather investing requires patience, discipline, and skill to grow wealth over time. Expressions that compare investing to gambling or magic, that it is scary or confusing, or "sport," are the words women too often choose when talking about investing. These pejoratives ignore the discipline of investing, a discipline women are well-equipped to master. Investing in stocks has been given a bum rap by women and this attitude is costing them future wealth.

WOMEN ARE NOT PLAGUED BY THE OVERCONFIDENCE MEN EXHIBIT, WHICH IS WHY THEY OUTPERFORM MEN

Brad M. Barber and Terrance Odean published a landmark research paper in 2001 entitled, "Boys Will Be Boys: Gender, Overconfidence, and Common Stock Investment," which analyzes the trading patterns of men and women over an extended period.[2] Their body of work is distinguished by the premise that women make better investors than men because they do not exhibit the overconfidence men tend to display when investing. Their findings? Men trade 45 percent more than women and generate returns on average about 1 percent less than women (3 percent less for single men when compared against single women). Barber and Odean attribute this finding to the results of previous psychological research, which shows that when it comes to finance men are more overconfident than women. Could this perhaps be why many women report feeling condescended to or even ignored in conversations with their financial advisors? Maybe. It may also be why we often shy away from investing. Yet, possessing a confidence level that is in check and building long-term focused portfolios with less trading (both common to women investors) are also the very attributes associated with better performance. Active trading may be what many women associate with investing when they identify the activity as "sport" or gambling. And in that regard they may be right. Barber and Odean in an article entitled, "Trading is Hazardous to Your Wealth" found that individual investors who actively trade "pay a tremendous performance penalty" for doing so. The active traders examined generated **portfolio turnover** of approximately 250 percent annually (which means that they sell and replace the assets in their portfolios 2.5 times per year) and produced an annual return of 11.4 percent versus the average individual investor who earned an annual return of 16.4 percent while generating portfolio turnover of 75 percent.[3] So it seems that women—inherently less confident than men and less inclined to trade—possess the very traits that produce superior investment returns. Another reason for their success might be women's willingness to do extensive amounts of research—more than one study cited this fact. But one organization, in particular, The National Council for Research on Women, gathered an extensive amount of research from around the globe and published a comprehensive study on "Women in Fund Management" in 2009.[4] The study concludes that women make decisions based on a more comprehensive collection of data and are willing to consider ideas that may be contradictory to their original assumptions. The study cites (among others) a Financial Times article by Celia Mather and published February 20, 2006, entitled, "Why Fund Management Suits the High-Achieving Women of Financial Services," which quotes Glenda Stone, co-chair of the UK Women's Enterprise Taskforce, "As investors, women do 60% more work than men before making a decision."

Add to all of the research cited another recent study conducted by author of *Man Down,* Dan Abrams in the "risk-on" hedge fund universe, which argues once again that women are outstanding investors. Between 2000 and 2009 the hedge funds managed by women returned 9.0 percent per year, compared to 5.8 percent for their male competitors.[5] Even when the appetite for risk and higher trading levels are factored in women still fare better.

The question begging to be asked is: why then don't we invest?

There seems to be something more than the right disposition or personality traits at work behind female success in investing. A consistent theme emerged as I culled the results of the research: women routinely identify a different purpose for their desire to accumulate wealth. Rather than viewing investing as a competition or a quest to beat a particular index, women are much more focused on meeting future financial goals for themselves and their families. Our financial priorities are different from men. We are interested in investing for personal goals including passing money on to heirs and, interestingly, not becoming a financial burden to our families. The Prudential study discussed earlier concludes that "this tendency to take care of others can compromise their families' futures." I disagree. It is not our tendency "to take care of others" first that will compromise our families' futures; rather, I would argue the risk lies in our lack of investment knowledge, which increases the very financial risk we are endeavoring to avoid.

A Successful Investment Discipline Requires Understanding How Markets Work and How We Respond to Market Forces

So, the good news is that women naturally enjoy the necessary traits of successful investors—discipline, a respect for risk (or an appropriate confidence level), and a willingness to invest for the long-term (lower levels of trading). But in order to establish an effective investment strategy we must understand the external factors that affect both the way the financial markets work and the way we respond to them. **Behavioral economics** theory developed by Amos Tversky and introduced in 1974 in his groundbreaking paper with Daniel Kahneman, "Judgment under Uncertainty: Heuristics and Biases" considers the decisions we make when faced with incertitude.[6] Many of the principles are directly applicable to the lack of certainty faced by individual investors each day. Tversky argues that our biases reveal some heuristics (problem-solving methods) that influence our judgments under uncertainty. These three factors are what Tversky calls representativeness: availability and adjustment and anchoring.

BEHAVIORAL ECONOMICS EXPLORES HOW OUR BIASES ARE COMPOUNDED BY RANDOM OR UNRELIABLE DATA

"Representativeness" reflects our response to stereotypes, neglect of sample size, ignorance of probability theory, and overemphasis on the law of small numbers (sampling size). It also considers favorableness, which is our response to a favorable description. To me, the influence of favorableness creates a particular problem for investors. We have all experienced it. At a party, on the soccer sidelines, over lunch, or a cocktail a friend tells us about the great investment they've made: it's doubled in the last year (somehow the stock always doubles) and we should really take a look at it. Because most of us feel inadequate about our investing prowess we listen with great interest. Doubled! Not many stocks in my portfolio have doubled over the last year. Perhaps I *should* take a look at that stock (though I have no idea what the company does). Tversky concludes: "If people predict solely in terms of their favorableness of the description, their predictions will be insensitive to the reliability of the evidence and to the expected accuracy of the prediction." And this is the key point: "reliability of the evidence." Is your friend an expert? Can they present a cogent case for why the stock is the right investment for you? Other than the assertion that is has "doubled" over the last year, why should the stock continue to outperform? And why is it right for you? Perhaps the most important insight to the veracity of the claim: does your friend (with his or her newfound wealth) pay for lunch?

The same is true of stock market prognosticators and pundits who make table-pounding recommendations on television. Their unwavering confidence and dogmatic emphasis are persuasive but the "favorable description" they offer may or may not be "reliable" and may or may not be right for you. I learned years ago to watch the financial news networks for news and to mute the volume when the experts are hawking their ideas. This is not a derogative judgment—I have appeared on those very networks for many years—and the fact remains when I suggest a stock I am looking at a specific set of factors: valuation, time horizon, an expected rate of return that may not match your investing profile. I am considering my own objectives, not, necessarily, yours. For those of us who are new to investing and interested in learning and gathering new ideas, beware! We are potentially ripe for being misled by favorableness. In chapter 7 we will be exploring how and where we get our information (hint: it's not from friends at cocktail parties). But for now, let's take a look at another bias that can invade our decision-making process.

My example of the friend with the stock that "doubled" also introduces the bias created by a (too) small sample size (in this case a sample of one) and ignores the statistical concept of **reversion (or regression) to the mean**. If your eyes glaze over at the mere sound of statistical theory rest assured, I share your response. So allow me to take a crack at an illustration that will move us from statistical theory to real life. Reversion to the mean simply argues that an extreme event (a stock doubling in one year, losing ten pounds in a week) is likely to be followed by a less extreme event (that same stock returns 1 percent the following year, I gain one pound the following week). Reversion to the mean assumes there is a norm—normal performance for a stock, normal weight loss rate, normal behavior in our children—and when data points vary from that norm they will eventually revert to the norm, or mean. That's it. Remember that one principle and you will keep yourself from chasing your friend's latest stock "double" at just the wrong time or pursuing the latest dieting craze for that matter.

BEHAVIORAL ECONOMICS ALSO STUDIES THE EFFECT OF THE RECENCY OF A RISKY EVENT ON SUBSEQUENT FINANCIAL BEHAVIOR

As someone who has been investing the span of three decades, I can tell you where I was and what I was doing during the crash of 1987, the market rout of 1990 when Iraq invaded Kuwait, the minute the market re-opened after the terrorist attacks in the fall of 2001, and during the market melt-down of 2008. Interestingly I cannot pinpoint where I was nor what I was doing during the many market rallies I've experienced. Like most people I remember the negative events much more vividly than the pleasant ones. I can't say why that is but I suspect we are all the same: when the market rises we accept it like we do a safe flight or our car performing as expected. When the market declines we are reminded of the harsh reality—that markets like airline travel, for example, contain risk—inherent risk—that we often take for granted.

The point, however, is that I have seen the harsh corrections and experienced the subsequent rallies (think of the forest fire that thins an overpopulated forest to make way for new growth). Those events are included in my investing sample. In other words, my investing sample includes more than one market event and that gives me confidence but, more importantly, my memory includes more than the recent effects of the financial crisis of 2008. The devastation of the 2008 crisis is palpable to many of us. We remember the gut-wrenching declines in our retirement accounts, the despair of wondering whether we would ever recover our losses, or be able to retire at all. But, **recency effect** is dangerous on both the downside and upside. How this information informs us and particularly women who are generally averse to risk is important to consider.

When subjected to recency effect what most investors forget is the concept we learned earlier in this chapter: reversion to the mean. If a market is rising or falling, the longer it does so the greater the probability it will cease doing so, or revert to the mean return. If we are able to consider the magnified impact of recent market trends on our behavior or at the very least our optimism or pessimism about the markets we might make better decisions as investors. And if we further factor in the statistical probability that, bar a significant worldwide disaster, eventually markets will revert to their mean return we will have the confidence to sit tight for the long-term.

VIEWING THE MARKETS OVER THE LONG-TERM PROVIDES MUCH BETTER INFORMATION THAN THE MOST RECENT EVENT

Jeremy Siegel, author of *Stocks for the Long Run* and the Russell E. Palmer Professor of Finance at the Wharton School routinely contributes historical long-term performance data to *Barron's*. A May 13, 2013 article outlines his research concluding that over every 30-year rolling period since 1871, the median return for stocks is 9.22 percent per year.[7] For 20-year rolling periods, the median performance is 8.09 percent. Note that over the rolling 30- and rolling 20-year periods in the last 140 plus years there is not a single negative return. A rolling period measurement is the most relevant because it replicates how we live and invest. In summary, a rolling 30-year measurement, for example, means that year 1 plus 29 years comprises the first rolling 30-year period, year 2 plus 29 years equals the second rolling 30-year period, year 3 plus 29 years, the third, and so forth. Over every one of those rolling 30-year periods since 1871, the median return for stocks has been 9.22 percent per year. Over the shorter, rolling 20-year measurements the market has returned on average 8.09 percent per year. These rolling periods include all the big bear markets—even the stock market crash of 1929—and still the market has returned 8.09 percent over each rolling 20-year period and 9.22 percent for each rolling 30-year period measured since 1871. Investing for the long-term produces solid, even enviable returns.

Consider the mathematical rule of 72. Assuming the rolling 30-year average return of 9.22 percent and employing the rule of 72 (which helps investors determine how quickly their investment will double at a given return), we would double our investment every 7.8 years. Compare that to the 2 percent saving rate we used in our earlier example. Our investment, in that scenario, would take 36 years to double.

Of course the stock market goes up and down during those rolling periods and sometimes it goes down a great deal. But what we learn by studying the history of the markets is that over time—if we follow and stick to our discipline—we will enjoy a mean return of around 9 percent per year. That is a historical fact. Siegel's work shows definitively that over every rolling 30-year period since data became available for stock returns in 1871—stocks have returned an average of 9.22 percent per year. Every rolling 30-year period. 9.22 percent.

I have summarized three behavioral principles researched in Tversky's work (favorableness, sample size, and recency effect). There are certainly more, though I believe these are the most important, but the critical thing to recognize when investing is that we come with personal and experiential biases that we can overcome—as long as we are aware of them. Personally, I have a recurring battle with recency effect. I counter it by reminding myself of what I know about the historical performance of the markets and their inevitable reversion to the mean.

In the Face of Uncertain Markets It Is Prudent to Be Aware of Our Biases When Honing Our Approach to Investing; Adding a Little Discipline Won't Hurt

The final element women bring to the investing table is discipline. Whether you are a professional woman or a stay-at-home mom, working two jobs outside the home or the dozen jobs you manage within the home, in order to get done what you have to accomplish each day requires discipline. Discipline, of course, comes in various forms. When I was a working mother I had to exert discipline over my usage of time; as a stay-at-home mother I still needed to focus on time discipline but spending discipline became much more critical. As I aged, I had to alter my discipline when it came to food. Less of some foods, more of others. My workout regimen changed, which also required discipline. When my kids left home I learned a new discipline—when to help out and when to let them fail. The point is, women's lives are filled with demands on our time, our bodies, our emotions, and our patience. Developing and maintaining discipline is inherent in our response to almost every job we have to complete, every choice we need to make. It must also form an integral part of our investment strategy.

Intelligent Investing Rule #2: *Don't run with the fast crowd: Establish a discipline that meets your objectives. Never chase total return and never, never, never buy a stock in a company you do not understand or does not meet your risk and investing objectives.*

LEARNING TO LEVERAGE OUR NATURAL AND ACQUIRED EXPERTISE IS A GOOD PLACE TO START

Women possess the inherent traits proven to produce solid investment performance. We understand discipline. The research repeatedly shows that we produce performance that is superior to men's by just about 1 percent per year. In short: we approach investing with excellent raw material. Behavioral economics provides us with a window into our own behavioral biases as risk-takers. Understanding and mastering our biases will allow us to mold our raw material, making us better investors. And acquiring historical knowledge of market performance provides us with the assurance required to stay the course during times of market stress.

Before we decide on an investment strategy let's take care of some housekeeping and develop an understanding of our financial goals. Establishing clear goals will further inform our investment strategy.

CHAPTER 3

In Order to Get There We Need to Know Where We Are Going: Establishing Financial Goals Informs Successful Savings and Investment Plans

Perhaps the reason many of us don't identify our financial goals is because the process is downright scary. We read predictions that college tuition will soon reach $100,000 per year, hear warnings that we will need $1 million or much more to support our retirement lifestyle, and entertain speculation that government easing will reduce the value of the dollar and eventually devour the majority of our savings. Don't count on Social Security if you are under 55, we are also told, because the trust fund is running out of money. So when it comes time to sit down and put pencil to paper, we freeze. The task is too big; the savings required, seemingly insurmountable. We'll have to worry about that tomorrow. Then suddenly it is tomorrow and the kids are heading off to college with a backpack full of loans and we are left wondering how we will manage to retire, if at all. The time to plan and save is always now.

Goals-based investing is nothing other than establishing separate objectives for separate life events rather than investing simply to beat an arbitrary index. Retirement, sending children off to college, charitable giving, a second home, weddings, a grand vacation are all events that require capital and should be considered in a goals-based investment plan. Our first step is to identify those events. Our second is to try to determine how we will provide for each activity. One of the easiest ways to plan for each of these events is through mental accounting.

MENTAL ACCOUNTING IS A GOOD PLACE TO BEGIN IN ESTABLISHING AND SAVING FOR OUR GOALS

Most of us have more than one life goal. Consequently, we need to establish a plan for each and may end up allocating various pools of money since each goal requires a slightly different plan. Retirement forty years in the future calls for one plan; college education for your Kindergartener thirteen years hence requires an entirely different plan. These discreet pools of money with diverse plans may sound confusing but the concept doesn't have to be. Behavioral finance experts refer to this as mental accounting. Mental accounting allows us to compartmentalize the various pools of money we set aside for specific purposes. Whether we establish separate accounts for each goal (as I did) or simply allocate portions within a larger account, our financial objectives each represent a different time horizon and require a corresponding level of risk based on the factors unique to each investment. This may include the length of time until the event, how much money will be invested initially, and the rate of contribution to fund the goal. Mental accounting gets us started and forces us to segment our savings plan and customize our investment plan accordingly.

Think of it simply. Establishing goals and setting the money aside for specific events is much like the budgeting plan employed by the dear mother of my lifelong friend. Each month she takes her disposable income for the month and allocates the appropriate amount to each activity or goal important to her. Each of those activities requires a different amount of money and is represented by a separate, labeled envelope. And each of those envelopes she carries with her to ensure she doesn't spend more than budgeted for each activity (think: grocery shopping, gas money, coffee with friends, Christmas gifts for the grandkids). What behavioral economists call mental accounting is for her a literal and highly effective strategy. At the end of the month whatever is left over in each envelope she adds to her savings "envelope." Mental accounting is simply segmenting our money into various investment accounts we've established for various goals. And because each goal is different, each goal requires a unique plan.

Let's take a look at a hypothetical example of mental accounting when considering future college needs.

Young Family: Both spouses are 30 years old and have just purchased a new home. Much of their disposable income is going to furnishings and now that they are expecting their first child they will be adding all the attendant expenses for a new baby. Both work and contribute the maximum allowed for retirement in their company plan as well as through IRA contributions.

At a dinner with friends they realize they need to establish a college savings account for their child. They go through the mental accounting of their income and expenses and determine they can set aside $200 per month for college. The couple researches the options and decides to establish a 529 College Savings Plan, which is like an IRA for education purposes—dividends and capital gains accumulate tax free—and is available at their broker for no fee. They discover 529 plans require the user to invest in funds provided by the sponsor of the plan—in this hypothetical example: Charles Schwab. Young Family muses over the college choices available to their child. They would like her to be able to attend a private school. Schwab offers a cost calculator on their 529 plan website where the couple plugs in their estimated monthly savings of $200. They choose an aggressive investment strategy. The Schwab college cost calculator takes into account the future amount of private college tuition and the appreciation of the $200 per month contributed and invested in the aggressive strategy over the subsequent eighteen years. The calculator determines that Young Family would accumulate $89,000 by the time their child is ready for college, leaving them $500,000 short; the future cost of a four-year private college is estimated by the calculator at approximately $625,000 after inflation. Whether that number proves to be true or not eighteen years hence, even at current private college tuition rates of approximately $30,000 to $50,000 per year, Young Family comes up short. Knowing that will allow them to either increase their monthly education savings or modify their education objective. Maybe a four-year state school will do just fine. They may adjust their mental accounting and decide to slow down the accumulation of household goods or even adjust their retirement saving to free up more cash to invest for college. Or they may decide to do neither but now, at least, they know where they stand and where they are going. Decisions like determining how much to save for college and how aggressively to invest those funds are dynamic and interdependent but each can only be made if the goals are established in the first place. Young Family may be not yet be meeting their goals but they are much more likely to do so now that they are aware of what is required and can adjust their savings and investment plan accordingly.

The question for Young Family becomes less about investing to beat an arbitrary market index, the traditional focus of most investors, and more about the combination of inputs required to meet family goals. Even by saving what they thought was a significant amount of money each month and investing it fairly aggressively the couple learned they needed to do more and, perhaps, modify their mental accounting and savings and investment objectives.

My family began our college saving program early on. When our kids became old enough we began talking to them about college and saving for college. If they added to the pot with babysitting, lawn mowing, or birthday money we matched it. Although we were unable to employ a 529 plan (the plan came into effect too late for us) we were able to establish custodian accounts for each child at our discount broker and managed the accounts ourselves. As the time drew close for them to attend college we talked about the purpose of the funds and and the fact that they would be able to keep whatever they did not spend on college for a home or whatever they chose in the future. Our son attended the US Naval Academy at Annapolis (which is a full scholarship university) so his funds continue to grow for future goals he may establish for his own family. Our daughter, on the other hand, decided to go to a private college where she received a basketball and academic scholarship that covered about half her tuition. She graduated with a little over half her funds intact and we continue to invest it for her future family goals.

Our savings weren't sacrificial—as I have already mentioned, we could have, with a little discipline saved more—but we did save and, more importantly, invested. And because the 529 plan, which is tax-advantaged, was not available we invested in a taxable environment that meant gains were taxed at our (the parents') ordinary income. The 529 removes the tax burden we incurred but, even still we accumulated enough to provide our children with the flexibility to choose and attend college. And so can you.

Someday You Will Retire and If You Are Like Most Women You Intend to Do So without Becoming a Burden to Your Family

The most memorable research statistic I've encountered states that a majority of women do not want to become a financial burden to their families. While women are generally confident in their ability to buy a home and take care of their own parents, they are not nearly as confident in their ability to have enough money to retire and maintain their lifestyle, according to the 2012–2013 Prudential Research Study entitled, "Financial Experience and Behaviors Among Women."[1] But, women are not alone in that fear. *The Wall Street Journal* cited the results of a 2012 study sponsored by Ameriprise Financial (and conducted by Koski Research) that interviewed 1,000 employed adults with investable assets of $100,000.[2] When asked if they were confident about being able to afford retirement, 46 percent said yes. The disconnect occurred when those same individuals were asked if they expected to be "extremely happy later in life" and 78 percent said yes. Though less than half believed they were prepared for retirement, over three-quarters believed they would be extremely happy in retirement. The discrepancy continued when the participants were asked if they were confident of having enough disposal income to travel and buy "extras" in their retirement years. Thirty-eight percent were confident but 72 percent said their ideal retirement would include taking "really nice" vacations. Expectations clearly do not match planning for most of us. Fidelity Investments recommends that individuals—conservatively—should plan to accumulate retirement assets that equal eight times their ending annual salary by age 67. It is no wonder that many Americans and many women, in particular, do not feel adequately prepared for retirement.

At the risk of sounding like that old cliche, the broken record, I'll say again: the only solution to our worries over retirement is to save more now and invest. In chapter 1 we were introduced to the concept of behavioral economics and UCLA professor, Dr. Benartzi, whose work reveals that "Only 1 out of 10 Americans is saving enough for retirement." Immediate gratification or the desire to spend now is one of the primary reasons he cites. But Benartzi offers two additional reasons. One is "inertia" or what I characterize as foot dragging. We understand the importance of saving for retirement and we intend to save, we really do. But we forgot about Little League sign-ups when we planned our budget and how could we know the microwave would break? We'll simply have to re-direct our savings into those projects this month. And so it goes. But there is a third reason that Benartzi refers to as "aversion to loss," which he correlates with the notion that people feel like they are losing money when they are prohibited (by saving) from spending it.[3] This is an interesting topic and not entirely unsupported by the broader research on behavioral economics. But, I believe the real focus on loss goes one step further. Investors, and especially women investors, may not like uncertainty but they hate actually losing money even more. Recall the behavioral economics pioneer Amos Tversky (on whom Benartzi bases a good deal of his theory). In 2001, Dr. Tversky argued, "It is not so much that people hate uncertainty—but rather, they hate losing." Tversky is not referring to losing as defined by Benartzi, where losing is the equivalent of being deprived of spending, but actually losing money; ending up with less than we started with. Based on my experience it is this unwillingness to lose money that impacts most financial decisions. I hear this fear articulated by women all the time. It goes something like this: *I am afraid of losing my money in the stock market. Rather than lose, I simply won't play.* Tversky and Kahneman developed this concept in greater depth in their landmark paper on what they called prospect theory in 1979.[4] They concluded that investors were not focused on risk as much as they were focused on losing money; investors might be willing to take more risk than was previously understood but they were much less willing to lose their hard-earned savings.

If women are indeed worried about retirement and about not becoming a burden to their children then the only solution is to save and to invest. We must stop worrying about losing. Inevitably, we will experience declines in the performance of our assets and we may undershoot our goal, but with a savings and investment plan we will hit closer to the mark. When I began in the investment business many corporations offered their employees traditional pension or **defined-benefit plans**. In these plans the company took on the risk of providing a defined-*benefit* to employees when they retired. The company paid all the expenses associated with the fund, was responsible for the investment of the funds, and for providing a fixed monthly pension payment to the employee upon retirement. The liability for employee retirement rested on the company. But as the workforce became more mobile and individuals were less inclined to remain at the same employer long enough to vest in their pension, the 401(k), a portable, employee-driven retirement plan, gained in popularity. Soon traditional pension plans were all but eliminated (though still offered to government employees and perhaps a tiny residual of corporate America) and individuals were offered participation in **defined-contribution plans** like the 401(k). In the process, employees received portability and the corporations were able to offload the responsibility of providing a fixed benefit to retirees in the future. Companies were also able to pass the responsibility for selecting the right asset allocation plan to the employee as well as some of the costs (participants often pay the fees of the funds they invest in). 401(k) plans raised the stakes for individuals to become informed investors of their retirement assets. Becoming better informed and more involved in our retirement investing sets us up to be better prepared for retirement. And less likely to become a burden to those we love.

Just as there are education cost calculators there are plenty of retirement planning calculators that consider your years to retirement, contributions, and investment performance. The information is readily available. What we do with it is what matters.

THE RIGHT ASSET ALLOCATION IS IMPORTANT TO MEETING OUR FINANCIAL GOALS

I am not pretending that making an asset allocation decision for each of our financial goals is easy. In fact, most of my accounts look surprisingly similar when it comes to asset allocation and remarkably unchanged over the last ten years. Which means I am similar to most investors. A 1998 study by the Employee Benefit Research Institute and Investment Company Institute reveals, "approximately 75% of 401(k) investors had not changed their equity allocations the previous two years." This is potentially problematic. Roger G. Ibbotson and Paul D. Kaplan in their paper, "Does Asset Allocation Policy Explain 40, 90, or 100 Percent of Performance?" demonstrate that about 40 percent of our performance is obtained through our asset allocation decision and 60 percent will come from our stock selection.[5] Asset allocation matters. So how do we ensure we are making the best allocation decisions to achieve our future goals?

A study conducted by TIAA-CREF in 1998 entitled, "Investing for a Distant Goal: Optimal Asset Allocation and Attitudes toward Risk" compared attitudes about risk and how those attitudes might affect optimal asset allocation.[6] The most informative part of the study displayed three asset allocation models set forth by three prominent financial experts: Jane Bryant Quinn, Burton Malkiel, and Jack Bogle. Each offered suggested allocations to equities based on years to the retirement event (Table 3.1).

Quinn's allocation model was the most aggressive, recommending 100 percent allocation to stocks when retirement is 30–40 years away and as much as 80 percent when retirement is less than 10 years away. Malkiel was the most conservative and Bogle, as you can see, in between. Any one of these allocations provide a reasonable approach to asset allocation as we establish investment

Table 3.1   Recommended stock allocations for future goals

Strategist	40 years to goal	30 years to goal	10 years to goal	Less than 10 years to goal
Malkiel	70%	60%	60%	50%
Bogle	80%	80%	70%	70%
Quinn	100%	100%	80%	80%

plans for each of our goals. But it might also be of interest to examine how each strategy performed over a theoretical 40-year period. The TIAA-CREF researchers employed the average real equity return of 9.2 percent (which was provided by Ibbotson based on stock returns from 1926–1995 and 2.5 percent for treasury bonds, based again on Ibbotson's work) and calculated returns for each asset allocation strategy. The retiree began with no balance but made a $5,000 annual contribution to her account and was set to retire in 40 years. The investor's end goal was set at $1 million by the time of retirement 40 years hence. Based on TIAA-CREF's calculations the Quinn allocation model resulted in a balance of $1,484,000, Bogle: $1,163,000, Malkiel: $859,000, a 100 percent constant equity allocation for the entire 40-year period: $1,867,000, and a 100 percent bond allocation: $348,000.

We can see from the results the impact of asset allocation on total return. It is significant. Conventional wisdom suggests that investors reduce exposure to stocks as they near their event date but we see the most compelling returns among the most aggressive allocations to stocks even as retirement age approaches. And we see that a constant 100 percent exposure to stocks over the 40-year period performs best of all. These results will vary somewhat, of course, depending on the period during which they are measured. But over the long-term, no matter the period examined, the trends and the performance relationship of each allocation model to the others will remain about the same. The most important fact, however, is that we have a guideline for allocation of our goals-based portfolios and we have an understanding of how those allocations might perform under certain circumstances. Asset allocation is within our reach. With a little effort we can establish plans of our own. But for those who still aren't comfortable, life-cycle funds are available.

Life-cycle Funds Are Designed for Investors Who Are Unwilling to Establish Their Own Investment Or Asset Allocation Plans

Life-cycle funds were primarily designed for defined contribution or 401(k) plans to address the problem of investors who are unwilling or, perhaps, unable to determine the most appropriate asset allocation of their own retirement assets. These strategies are not necessarily designed to maximize total return but, rather, to balance risk against return over the long-term. The funds typically take into account the number of years participants have until retirement, often naming the funds with potential retirement dates such as the 2015 fund or the 2030 fund. The longer investors have until retirement, the more the funds are invested in **growth assets** like stocks. Life-cycle funds for investors with fewer years until retirement are populated more heavily with **protection-seeking** investments like bonds. In theory, the strategy makes perfect sense.

But what happens when market conditions deteriorate rapidly as they did in 2008–2009? Critics argue that in a declining market environment those closest to retirement who are invested in life-cycle funds take on unintended risk. If growth assets (stocks) are declining significantly the investor should make a conscious decision regarding their exposure to the asset class. They may want to sell or, perhaps, add to their holdings as stocks decline but the fund allocation remains in the hands of the investment manager and is fixed according to the preestablished asset allocation formula. No adjustments in response to market conditions can be made. Conversely, critics argue, if a bull market is raging and an investor (again close to retirement) is hardly exposed to growth assets, then the opportunity cost is significant. They are giving up too much in terms of potential return. The paradox is that investors are unwittingly taking on too much or too little risk in life-cycle funds no matter the economic environment. All of which makes my point. If you do not take responsibility for managing the wealth you are accumulating for retirement you run the extreme risk of compromising your long-term total return or worse yet, taking on unintended risk. The purpose of the life-cycle funds seems to ignore what behavioral economics tells us about investors' willingness to sustain risk as long as they don't lose. The more intentional we are in implementing our investment strategy and our investment plan and the more engaged we are in the process, the more likely we are to grow our wealth and meet our goals.

UNPLANNED WINDFALLS CAN BE A BLESSING BUT YET ANOTHER BIG DECISION: TO DOLLAR-COST AVERAGE OR NOT TO DOLLAR-COST AVERAGE

Unplanned windfalls can be life changing but they, too, require careful planning as we determine how and when to invest the funds. Many studies have been conducted on the benefits of **dollar-cost averaging** the funds into the market or lump-sum investing the assets in one fell swoop. Dollar-cost averaging (DCA) is much like my approach to getting into the pool. I am an incher, an incrementalizer, a toe-dipper, if you will. I slowly work my way in, agonizing step by agonizing step, despite the fact that I know if I simply dove in I would be acclimated to the water temperature in a matter of seconds. Still, I inch. DCA employs a similar strategy when investing a large sum into stocks by inching into the market. DCA strategies vary and you can easily design your own but the process involves investing predetermined amounts of money into the market over regular, predefined intervals. DCA makes us feel better about investing in the face of uncertainty. And let's face it, most investing involves uncertainty. If the market has been strong we often hesitate to invest all at once because we worry we are buying in at the top just in time for stocks to decline. If the market is weak we worry it will continue to decline and we will lose our money. By averaging into the market we are creating a natural hedge. DCA is like buying insurance when the dealer shows an ace in Blackjack. We would rather give up some of our gains to insure against a loss because we don't like to lose. The most relevant, real-life example of dollar cost averaging is the investment of our 401(k). Via our monthly contributions we average our way into the market over time. The same is true of all our financial goals as we save and invest, save and invest.

The research consistently shows that lump-sum investing outperforms DCA about two-thirds of the time. That is not surprising considering that the long-term trend of the stock market is up and, therefore, being invested produces better returns than not being invested. Additionally the S&P 500 has generated positive results in over 70 percent of the years from 1926 through 2010. But the research also shows that investors feel a good deal better when they spread the risk over time through DCA. If you find yourself in the happy predicament of receiving a windfall consider the performance benefits of lump-sum investing, factor in the psychic and risk reduction benefits of DCA, and, of course, mentally account for your life goals as you determine your asset allocation and make your decision about whether to dollar-cost average or invest your lump sum at once.

Intelligent Investing Rule #3: *Establish your life goals early and stick to your plan. If you think it's hopeless because you've waited too long, remember: The time to save is always now. It is never too late. And remember, too, the only way to "lose" is to not invest at all.*

OUR LIFE GOALS SHOULD BE IMPORTANT ENOUGH TO COMMAND A REASONABLE AMOUNT OF OUR ATTENTION: THE ONLY WAY TO AVOID "LOSING" IS TO ENSURE WE ARE INTELLIGENTLY IN THE GAME

Focusing on investing for our own goals and those we establish for our family raises the odds we will attain those goals. We gain an understanding of how much we need to save and, more importantly, the necessity to be invested to achieve our goals. The stock market offers no guarantee of return simply because we are paying attention, but knowledge and involvement provide the opportunity to manage our risk and to avoid the behavioral tendencies that exacerbate underperformance. It's time to take a look at valuation measures that allow us to discern when stocks are reasonably priced. In short it is time to hone our investment discipline, our personal investment strategy, and begin identifying great companies at reasonable prices that will move us closer to achieving our life goals.

CHAPTER 4

Developing an Investment Discipline That Will Achieve Our Goals: For the Diligent Student and Practitioner, Investing— Like Any Skill—Can Be Perfected; Matching Our Investment Strategy with Our Goals Is Paramount

Over my thirty years as a professional investor I've heard every cocktail party stock tip and market timing success imagined; I've come to understand that with one hand wrapped around a highball, everyone's a winner. Yet, if we listened to every hot tip or changed direction in the midst of big market moves based on casual advice advocated by friends or acquaintances, we would likely chase our tales right into bankruptcy. The only sure way to ensure we really do win over time is to stay the course we establish based on our personal and family objectives and to acknowledge that no investor or investment discipline can, or will, be right during every short-term period. If we adopt a strategy that lines up with our long-term goals and our investing temperament we are much more likely to succeed. So let's begin by acquainting ourselves with the two primary stock investment style categories: growth and value.

GROWTH AND VALUE INVESTORS HAVE DISTINCT PERSONALITY BIASES

Are you an early adapter? Did you own the first release of the iPhone or iPad or are you sure to be in line for the newest blockbuster movie? If so, you are likely to be comfortable buying growth stocks. Growth stock investors are trendsetters. They are risk takers who are comfortable investing in new, innovative products and companies—think Facebook, Twitter, or Tesla Motors today or the legendary growth stories like Wal-Mart, Starbucks, or Apple Computer of yesterday. And they are less focused on the price of the stock than they are on the price *momentum* of the stock. Earnings growth in excess of the rate of growth of most other stocks is the growth stock investor's primary measure of attractiveness. Going *with* the crowd is another defining characteristic. Being nimble, a must.

Value stock investors on the other hand are somewhat more reticent and conservative by nature. Though not necessarily risk averse, value investors wait for products to develop into premier brands or companies to become established, stable growers before they jump in. If you still carry a flip phone, for example, you likely share some of the attributes of the value investor. Or if you drive your car, as I did, to the point of deafening rattles with yards of electrical tape holding the side-view mirror in place, so you could sweep into the car dealership on the last day of the year and secure a deal, you are someone who cares about price. Being a value investor does not necessarily make you boring (though you will have little to contribute to the cocktail party chatter) but, rather, being a value investor makes you prudent, price sensitive; careful. Going against the crowd feels natural to the value investor, holding the stocks of great companies for the long-term, a hallmark.

Both growth and value stock investing can be successful. The fabled Peter Lynch of Fidelity's Magellan Fund was the epitome of a successful growth stock investor. His book *One Up on Wall Street* advocates the notion we are exploring here: that average investors can invest as well as or better than professional money managers simply by looking for companies with products we know and use in our everyday lives. "Everyone," says Lynch, "has the brainpower to follow the stock market. If you made it through fifth grade math, you can do it." Warren Buffett, on the other hand, is considered the quintessential value investor (though he eschews labels—more about that in chapter 5). Buffett is known for his homey commentary but like a clever, self-deprecating, country lawyer his advice is shrewd and wise: "It is far better to buy a wonderful company at a fair price than a fair company at a wonderful price." The celebrated growth manager and the celebrated value manager have both made billions of dollars for their respective clients. And both have implemented strategies that are compatible with their personalities and skills. As should you.

When examined closely the differences between growth stock investing and value stock investing are more nuanced than many managers admit. Both types of investors are interested in making money and the only way to do so is to sell a stock for more than you pay for it. The difference lies in the investor's focus. Where growth managers are interested in the potential growth of the company, its products, and earnings, they are often willing to pay up for exceptional growth, while value managers—though not indifferent to growth—are much more interested in the price they pay for that growth. The growth investor believes if she pays a little too much for a stock, the company's rapid growth will soon redeem her through rapid price appreciation. The value investor, on the other hand, would rather buy stocks in great companies with depressed stock prices even if she has to wait a little longer for growth to return. Her emphasis is on the quality of the company's products and the management team, which will eventually return the company to a reasonable growth rate, resulting in price appreciation.

An Encouraging Word for Women about Understanding and Selecting an Investment Style

Obviously there are other considerations besides personal bent when selecting an investment style. Presumably you are reading this book because you are one of the majority of women who self-identify as lacking in financial knowledge or who characterize themselves as risk averse. And further suppose you are like most women whose lives are filled with interruptions. The foremost consideration must be not only what suits your personality but your ability to invest the time and focus required for whichever investment discipline you ultimately choose. Or you will eventually throw up your hands in surrender. And that would be a failure for all of us because the goal of this book and my personal passion is to equip women with the tools required to achieve financial security. The objective we are working toward is to establish a discipline that is practically implementable and will allow you to meet your future financial goals. Our very first Intelligent Investing Rule stated: *Having any discipline is better than no discipline.* If we get it mostly right that is infinitely better than not participating at all.

In 1968 Matina Horner completed her groundbreaking research on women's fear of success in high achievement conditions.[1] Horner's hypothesis was that women's fear of success inhibited their ability to achieve, what she called "negative success imagery." We are four decades removed from her findings and the women I know juggle complex lives in a high-achieving and stressful environment. We have succeeded and we have succeeded in overcoming out potential "fear of success." Any "negative imagery" we may have concocted around investing needs to be disabused. Investing, too, is well within our grasp and abilities. Hang in there. We are about to sink our teeth into the meat of investing.

Before we examine the growth and value styles in greater depth, let's look at what the research reveals about the two investing style categories.

WHAT THE RESEARCH TELL US ABOUT VALUE VERSUS GROWTH STOCK INVESTMENT PERFORMANCE

Mountains of data have been crunched in an effort to determine which style of investing—value versus growth—is the most compelling over the long-term. The definitive study is one conducted by Eugene F. Fama (Graduate School of Business, University of Chicago) and Kenneth R. French (Sloan School of Management, Massachusetts Institute of Technology) entitled, "Value versus Growth: The International Evidence."[2] The abstract to the 1998 research report states: "Value stocks have higher returns than growth stocks in markets around the world. For the period of 1975 through 1995...value stocks outperform growth stocks in twelve of thirteen major markets." And the average annual return differential is over 7.5 percent—that is: value stocks outperformed growth stocks by over 7.5 percent per year from 1975 to 1995 in twelve of thirteen major markets around the globe. Previous research conducted by "Lakonishok et al. (1994) and Haugen (1995) argues that the value premium...arises because the market undervalues distressed stocks and overvalues growth stocks. When these pricing errors are corrected, distressed (value) stocks have high returns and growth stocks have low returns."[3,4] Fama and French's research confirms that view: buying stocks with distressed prices results in significant outperformance over time.

In 2003 Ibbotson Associates conducted a similar study that also examined the performance of growth versus value stocks from 1969 through December 2002.[5] But the Ibbotson study examined value and growth stocks in eight categories: micro-capitalization value and growth, small-capitalization value and growth, mid-capitalization value and growth, and large-capitalization value and growth. The **market capitalization** of a company is simply the value of all the shares outstanding (held by investors) multiplied by the current stock price. This measure tells investors how big the company is. The four best performers during the period were all value stock categories: micro-, small-, mid-, and large-cap value. The four growth stock groups were the worst performers. The period examined included times when both growth and value styles performed well, and still over the entire period value stocks of all sizes significantly outperformed growth stocks. It would seem then that owning value stocks leads to significant outperformance in markets around the world over almost any time period and in any size category or market capitalization level available to investors.

Based on historical performance alone we may then decide that value investing makes the best sense for our portfolio but what if growth stock investing seems to match our investing temperament and goals? Is it ever possible for the value investor to own growth stocks and still generate the value style outperformance? Glad you asked. Buying growth stocks at a reasonable price is the value investor's trump card as we will discover in chapter 5. For now, a quick review.

A Quick Recap

In chapter 2 we learned why women make excellent investors. If those attributes: a lack of overconfidence, a willingness to do the research, a desire to provide for family goals are consistent with your personal characteristics, they should influence the investment discipline you ultimately establish. In chapter 3 we developed a deeper understanding of why and how to set life goals. Hopefully you have gone through the mental accounting process and, at the very least, established your goals and estimated the capital required to meet those goals. If you answered "yes" to my description of the traits of a growth manager but know that your lifestyle or schedule or risk aversion don't align with that strategy then by all means don't embrace growth investing simply because you happen to also be a trend setter. In other words, temperament matters but so does the fact of your family goals, the length of time until those goals become reality, and your ability to commit the varying amounts of time required to implement your investment discipline.

We are going to explore four style variations—two in this chapter, two in the next. They are: growth and value investing (which you've met briefly), a blended style—growth at a reasonable price, and a more passive, less research-intensive approach: indexed exchange-traded funds. Think of these four as templates. Each are entirely accessible to you and well within your investing purview. You may decide to choose a discreet discipline as outlined or a combination of any or all. I actually employ all four styles in my own portfolio.

With a deeper understanding of the style options you will possess the third leg in the financial tripod, the "how." We've addressed the "who": women make better investors; the "what": we invest to achieve our future family goals; and now the "how": a personal investment discipline that lines up with our natural abilities and helps us to get where we want to go.

Growth Investors Often Are on the Lookout for the Next Breakthrough Product Or Technology Company

Once a product becomes widely acclaimed many chide themselves for not having seen it coming. We may mourn the fact that we didn't buy the stock years or decades ago. If only we'd known. I'd be resting comfortably on a lakeside hammock had I purchased Costco stock when we began spending our life savings there. Or Nike for that matter. Apple, Wal-Mart, Nordstrom—all great growth companies—have returned generously to long-term holders. Why didn't I see it at the time? Because I wasn't looking. Great growth investors intuitively understand trends. Often product and tech junkies, they can tell you the best movies out and the ones to watch for; they know the trendiest new restaurants and the most useful or interesting website for finding whatever they are looking for. They employ social media to their advantage. Growth investors are plugged in. If you are one of those people, start looking around and paying attention. If you were a Chipotle junky from the get-go you could have considered not only buying another burrito bowl but a few shares of the stock. (You would be basking in your profits now.) If you can't survive without your Netflix account and were, perhaps, an early adapter of the service, you might have considered buying shares in the company. (If you did you probably wouldn't be feeling the need to read this book.) The point is if you had purchased either stock after the **initial public offering**—let's say the first full year after—you would have enjoyed returns of 835 percent and 6,588 percent respectively through the end of 2013.

But embedded in that strong performance is a great deal of risk. Often, the early years of outperformance for growth stocks are the most volatile, the period when the expectations are the greatest, when soaring growth is factored into investor expectations and reflected in the price of the stock. Take, for example, the performance of Netflix (**stock ticker:** NFLX) from 2011 to 2013. The stock price has flailed around like a lotto ball in a tornado. In 2011 Netflix stock rose to just over $300 then plummeted to the mid-$60 range in a matter of months. Back up to $120 it climbed only to landslide to the mid-$50 range, again in a matter of a few months. Then another inexorable climb to over $300 during the subsequent twelve months, finally closing out 2013 at $369.17 per share. And yet during that almost three-year period of excessive volatility NFLX produced an enviable cumulative return of 109.2 percent compared to 56.2 percent for the S&P 500.

Remember the concept of recency effect and its impact on investor psychology especially during periods of extreme volatility. There is no better explanation for why investors sometimes sell when they should be buying and buy when they should be selling. Our tendency is to remember a more recent experience better than a previous experience. When holding volatile growth stocks like Netflix the risk is that in an effort to increase our gains we may be tempted to add to holdings when the stock is near its highs and to sell after a collapse in price to avoid further losses. The growth investor requires a spine of steel and must have confidence in the company's prospects to stay the course or get out and stay out.

WHERE EARNINGS IN GROWTH STOCKS ARE ABSENT, LOOK TO THE PRICE-TO-SALES RATIO FOR VALUATION INFORMATION

Finding growth stocks is not difficult. They make headlines and are the kinds of companies receiving a great deal of air time on the financial news programs because they are often pioneering new product trends or technologies or, even more thrilling, developing new markets altogether. Consequently earnings are not as important to investors as sales. The company is expected to reinvest the revenues into future growth. Think of Amazon.com Inc. (**stock ticker:** AMZN) founded in 1994. The stock has appreciated 7,842.7 percent beginning the first full year since shares were first offered to the public in 1997. But earnings have been almost nonexistent while the company continues to gain share from its competitors. The earnings are so modest (in 2012 the company had a loss of $0.09 per share on sales of $134.86 per share or $61 billion in total) that many of the traditional stock valuation methods are essentially incalculable or irrelevant. What growth investors want to see from Amazon is sales growth and market share domination, so the most insightful valuation measure for a company like AMZN is one that can measure the company's effectiveness at growing sales—the **price-to-sales ratio** (p/s). This ratio simply quantifies the price per share an investor is paying for sales (or revenue) per share. Alone, the measure is merely a single data point but when compared to other similar stocks and Amazon's own historical p/s, the valuation tool can provide perspective on the attractiveness of AMZN stock; and all the necessary information is easily available and simple to calculate.* While p/s provides an insight into the cost of sales growth when earnings are either nonexistent or temporarily depressed, it should also be considered in light of the company's ability to historically grow sales and continue to grow sales in the future (estimates also easy to access). When these perspectives are analyzed, the p/s can be an effective and reliable tool for buying growth stocks.

Bloomberg.com is a good source of financial data and stock news. The p/s ratio is presented as well as a number of other valuation measures, financial news, and robust charting capabilities. Other sites like Yahoo Finance provide blogs specific to growth stocks and the latest, breaking news. Yahoo Finance is a comprehensive and convenient site—one of my favorite go tos—when I am researching a stock. See chapter 7 and the appendix for more stock research websites and ideas.

A recent examination of Amazon's p/s ratio demonstrates investors believe Amazon can continue to grow sales quite handily. While the stock price accelerated over the previous two years the p/s has bounced around in a fairly flat range. Ratios are sometimes difficult to intuitively grasp (but become easier with time). However, with the dramatic price movement of AMZN stock and a relatively flat p/s we can conclude that the lack of change in the ratio is due to the fact that sales are growing as quickly as the stock price. That's good. The danger lies in the circumstance where the p/s rises because the stock price rises faster than sales growth. That may be a signal to savvy growth investors to exit the stock. However, because p/s is a ratio it is important to examine the underlying numbers yourself. It takes little time compared to the value or protection you are creating in your portfolio.

A WARNING FOR BUSY WOMEN

Growth stock investing is highly dependent on **momentum**—the acceleration of a stock price or trading volume. The simple explanation for that acceleration is that the stock enjoys more buyers than sellers. Momentum (in either direction) can continue for a long time but when there is a sudden shift it is difficult for individual investors operating outside the cozy confines of Wall Street to react in a timely manner. Because these stocks move so quickly and dramatically growth investors must be nimble and willing to sell or buy quickly. Frequently there is no time for dollar-cost averaging. Your are either in or out. So, even if your temperament is oriented toward growth stock investing you must decide if your lifestyle will accommodate that kind of focus on your stock holdings. During the dotcom heydays a number of Internet stocks appreciated into the stratosphere and then crashed and burned at breathtaking speed. Company insiders who presumably have access to near perfect information got caught in the momentum shifts and went from paper millionaires to not, virtually overnight. The same trend that jet propels a stock up can turn on a dime and drive the price down. The reasons are less important than the head-snapping rapidity of the moves. For women who are busy managing lives, careers, and family, buying aggressive growth stocks may not be the most practical strategy. For now it is best to understand that if you choose to own the fastest-growing companies you will experience a good deal of volatility and inevitably some significant wins as well as losses. As an investor in truly leading-edge growth companies you must be willing to ignore the trail of switchbacks and climb straight up the face of the mountain. This style of investing is not for the faint of heart.

A PERSONAL CONFESSION ABOUT GROWTH STOCK INVESTING

Despite Amazon's performance and the value of employing the p/s ratio as a measure of value, I find stocks like AMZN befuddling. I am not pretending that the price performance has not been spectacular. It has. And I wish I could overlook my own investing discipline and buy the stock, but I can't. For me the one tangible in buying stocks—the principle I can hang my investing hat on—is company earnings. When there are no earnings, or erratic earnings, I don't have a playbook to work from. Analyzing the price-to-sales ratio certainly provides perspective but my investing discipline requires the companies I own to produce earnings. So, I will admittedly (and sadly) miss the great growth stories like AMZN. But I take comfort in the fact that the academic research we explored on value versus growth demonstrates that even without owning great growth stocks like Amazon, investors focused on a specific discipline like value investing will generate superior returns over time.

VALUE INVESTORS BELIEVE THAT EVENTUALLY GOOD THINGS HAPPEN TO BAD STOCKS OF GREAT COMPANIES

The first thing to understand about value investing is that the quality of the company and the value or price of the stock can be and, often is, diametrically opposed. Particularly at turning points. Just because a company's stock is what we might call a bad stock (one that has underperformed and is now cheap) does not mean that the company is a bad potential investment. Provided that it is a very good company that has simply hit a road bump and is out of favor with investors the depressed stock price may present a golden opportunity. The glitch may be temporary, due to an earning's miss or new product flop or a myriad of other mistakes. Bad news is the companion of investors who are interested in buying inexpensive stocks. Almost everyone can tell you why the company is cheap; they are not nearly as likely to tell you when it will cease being cheap. In fact, most investors won't start talking about the stock again—let alone buy it—until the problems have been fixed and the stock has appreciated well off the lows. This gap presents a potential opportunity for value-oriented investors who are comfortable going against the crowd and willing to buy the stocks of great companies when no one else likes them.

Traditional value stocks tend to be maturing companies. They are past the go-go growth days experienced early in their product or technology cycle and they are often financially well-managed, with a focus on enhancing earnings growth through cost-cutting and acquisitions in the face of slowing sales growth. These companies almost always pay a dividend to shareholders as a nod to their slower growth. And don't miss this: If stock price appreciation reflects what investors believe is sustainable earnings growth, the dividend reflects what *management* believes is sustainable earnings growth. And the dividend supplements investors' returns by paying them a kind of guaranteed, stable return in the form of an up-front dividend. But don't be confused. Dividend paying value stocks are not bond substitutes because dividends can (and do) grow unlike the coupon paid on a bond. With value stocks the investor expects not just future price appreciation in the stock (albeit, sometimes slower than the expected growth stock return) but also a growing dividend payment. In these companies dividends can contribute a significant portion of the expected return for the stock.

Twenty-plus years ago one of my colleagues made a presentation to a roomful of investment professionals about our method for identifying cheap stocks, which included a focus on dividend policy. After the presentation he engaged in a discussion with a university finance professor who finally declared, "Sorry, I just don't believe in dividends." My colleague was flummoxed by the response. Dividends are real, they don't require faith—they simply "are." Rather than approach the topic in an analytical fashion our professor friend seemed to approach investing as though it were a religion. Which is precisely the opposite of what we seek to do. Investing successfully requires a kind of agnostic thought process. We must be indifferent to emotion and the latest trend. Undogmatic, dispassionate, concerned only with the facts. The question is not whether we believe in dividends or not, the question is what they are telling us. Bias adds little to total return. We must deal with the world and stock market we are given. It is there we will find value if we seek it. It is there we collect dividends whether we believe in them or not. Don Kilbride, the manager of the Vanguard Dividend Growth fund recently told *Barron's* "Ninety percent of what we do is opinion—value, quality, estimates. But two (factors) are not debatable: Price and dividend. I focus as much as I can on fact."[6]

Excellent advice. In investing our objective is always to control the variables we can control.

Because the dividend is a significant portion of the expected total return, producing the earnings to pay the dividend is obviously important. So, it would be a mistake to assume that these maturing organizations are dead or dying. Think of value stocks as the shares of middle-aged companies that remain productive but are perhaps a little more deliberate, a little stiffer in the knees, a little jowlier, but still hearty. Maturing companies are still growing and they may grow at above-market levels once more, but until then the management team's commitment to the dividend is paramount.

There are many variables that affect stock prices—many out of our control—our objective is to control the variables we can control and one of those variables is the price. The second variable is the dividend. And as "The Grand Dame of Dividends," and newsletter publisher Geraldine Weiss reminds us, "Dividends don't lie." A reliable benchmark if ever there was one.

Intelligent Investing Rule #4: *Remain dispassionate but diligent. Almost anyone will be able to tell you what is wrong with a company when its stock is cheap. If we buy high-quality companies we can wait for the management team to solve the problems and restore earnings growth; in the meantime we are getting paid via the dividend for the fundamentals to improve.*

WHY DIVIDENDS MATTER TO VALUE INVESTORS AS A VALUATION TOOL

The best value stocks are those in which the management and the board express what I call a "dividend paying culture." By that I mean a culture where the dividend represents a portion of what they believe to be long-term sustainable earnings. This is important because if the management team views the dividend in the context of earnings, then whether they raise the dividend or not signals a great deal to us as investors. The "dividend paying culture" of a company can serve to provide investors with an insight into what the insiders (management and the board) believe long-term sustainable earnings power to be. With this insight we can be confident in the face of market neglect or pessimism. There are many examples of this dividend paying culture in US corporations though it is voiced in slightly different ways by managements of different companies in various industries. Below are a few recent examples of company comments on the dividend.

During the fall of 2013, AT&T's chief financial officer was quoted in *Barron's* as telling shareholders: "Our dividend is clearly a sacred matter for us." He went on to say, "We clearly understand as managers of AT&T the importance of our dividends to our shareholders." Sometimes, the dividend policy is implied.[7] Take Honeywell International. In October 2013 the company raised the quarterly dividend 10 percent. *Barron's* reported: "That's the fourth hike in three years, and it will add $126 million or thereabouts to yearly payouts . . . Honeywell has paid dividends every year since 1887."[8] Now, that's a dividend policy. Or this from the McDonald's Corporation 2012 Annual Report: "The Company has paid dividends on its common stock for 37 years and has increased the dividend amount every year." The report went on to say that the 10 percent increase in the dividend for 2012 "reflects the Company's confidence in the ongoing strength and reliability of its cash flow." And here is the important part: "As in the past, future dividend amounts will be considered after reviewing profitability expectations." Management and the board of directors is signaling to investors their level of confidence surrounding future earnings growth through their dividend policy. Over my thirty years as an investor I have found the dividend to be a very reliable way to look at value stocks.

Information about the dividend is easier to come by than you might think. A simple review of the company's online annual report will often reveal the company's dividend policy, but even if the policy is not articulated as clearly as the McDonald's dividend policy an investor can infer a great deal from the company's history of dividend payments and increases. This information can also be obtained on most free financial websites (reminder: see appendix for a comprehensive list of free financial websites). Not all value stocks pay a dividend but the majority do. Considering a company's dividend paying culture as manifested in the stock's dividend paying history and dividend growth is the first valuation criterion I consider when looking at a potential holding. The other ratios we have discussed and will discuss are additional factors I consider but this is where I start. I want to know what management knows about future earnings. Because, after all, earnings—whether now or in the future—are what we are buying when we buy stocks.

How Dividends Contribute to Total Return

Though I have read dozens of studies on the contribution of dividends to overall equity returns and have first-hand experience in owning these stocks (in some cases for decades), I am always startled by the magnitude of the impact of dividends on total return. It's not just that dividends contribute to investment performance; they contribute the majority of the total return produced. The compounding power of dividends is indisputable. In a 2003 editorial for the *Financial Analysts Journal* entitled, "Dividends and The Three Dwarfs," professional investor and author Rob Arnott examines the source of the total return for stocks over a 200-year period (1802–2002).[9] (Stock data dating back to 1802 is based on Schwert data, 1990.[10]) The average annual total return achieved is 7.9 percent (this average return differs from Dr. Jeremy Siegel's 9.2 percent average total return calculated for rolling thirty-year periods—the variation is due to the period measured and the fact that Arnott is considering annual performance not rolling year performance as Siegel does). Dividends plus the growth of those dividends (excluding the impact of inflation) account for 5.8 percent annually. In other words, of the 7.9 percent average annual return of stocks over the last 200 years, 5.8 percent or 73 percent of the return was due to dividends. Seventy-three percent!

And so it comes as no surprise that the higher yielding segments of the market perform better than the non-dividend paying segments. Heartland Funds published a white paper entitled, "Dividends: A Review of Historical Returns," which draws heavily on dividend quintile research conducted by Kenneth French (again of Fama and French fame). French's research considers the average return of non-dividend payers against five yield quintiles of stocks since 1924 through 2012.[11] The higher yielding quintiles (the fourth and fifth) outperform the lower quintiles (the first and second) as we would expect. But the top performers were the stocks in the fourth quintile, with an average annual return of 11.49 percent compared to the non-payers at 8.23 percent and the top yielding fifth quintile at 10.72 percent. Because the average individual does not necessarily view their investing time horizon as 84 years, French breaks the data down into 66 consecutive rolling twenty-year periods. Again the top performer is quintile 4, with a twenty-year average annual return of 13.4 percent compared to the non-payers at 10.17 percent and the highest-yielders in the fifth quintile at 13.08 percent.

Why do the highest yielding stocks perform worse than those in the fourth quintile? Heartland concludes and my actual experience confirms that sometimes the highest yielding stocks are signaling insurmountable problems. The dividend may be at risk because of deteriorating earnings. (At the first sign of the cut in the dividend paid by a company I am gone.) And, or, the stock has declined so much because of worries over the underlying business that the yield has risen to extraordinarily high levels, signaling looming bankruptcy or some other such disaster. But this is only sometimes and we will be examining warning signs for dividend risk in chapter 12. Suffice to say that focusing on dividend yielding stocks provides not only insightful valuation information but contributes significantly to our total return over time. All you have to remember is: 73 percent.

After completing the research for this chapter I altered the profile of my own investment portfolio to include the reinvestment of dividends paid by the company into that company's stock. Previously I had been deploying the dividend income when I saw fit, which means that sometimes I did and sometimes I didn't reinvest the income. But the research overwhelmingly shows that reinvesting dividend income works and it works spectacularly. So now my dividend reinvestment is automatic, not subject to my moods or whims, or worse, inevitable lack of focus. My dividends will be redeployed into each stock just as it was in my IBM example in chapter 1. Every quarter, whether I deserve it or not, the companies in the stocks I own pay me a dividend and I now reinvest that money right back into the underlying company stock. I don't have to think about whether now is the right time or not; my dividend reinvestment plan dollar-costs averages me into additional shares of companies I already know I want to own and based on hundreds of years worth of data I can rest in the confidence that over time I am employing a sound strategy. A win-win if I ever saw one.

The Dogs of the Dow

Investing in higher yielding stocks carries other benefits. Because expectations for these stocks have already been reduced, the price swings or **volatility** will be much lower. Traditional value stocks plod. And one of the most interesting group of plodders is the top ten highest yielding stocks that comprise the **Dow Jones Industrial Average** (DJIA) or the Dow. The Dow is an index of thirty major US corporations that was first calculated in 1896 and represents a broad swath of corporate America. These are industry leaders, the kinds of companies that tend to pay meaningful dividends.

In 1991 money manager Michael O'Higgins introduced a much replicated investment strategy employing the top ten yielding stocks in the DJIA, commonly called "The Dogs of the Dow." The strategy seeks to buy those top ten yielders at the beginning of the calendar year with an equal weighting in each stock (of 10 percent) and then readjust the holdings at the beginning of the next year to once more reflect the top yielding stocks. Buying the "Dogs" is easy and **tax efficient** (because you are only making adjustments once per year). And the strategy is estimated to have outperformed the Dow by about 3 percent since 1957. At the beginning of 2013 the ten highest yielding stocks in the Dow were AT&T, Verizon Communications, Intel Corporation, Merck & Co., Hewlett-Packard (which has since been removed from the DJIA and replaced), Pfizer, Inc., DuPont, General Electric, McDonald's Corporation, and Johnson & Johnson—well-known companies that are generally industry leaders. At the beginning of 2014, two names were added to the list: Cisco Systems and Microsoft. These stocks replaced DuPont and Johnson & Johnson who were removed because of strong performance and, therefore, declining yields.

The Dogs has detractors to be sure. And some of their criticism is valid. For example, we already know that owning the very highest yielding stocks carries some risk. But in the case of the Dogs these companies are not necessarily the highest yielding stocks in the entire market (the universe Fama and French measured) but simply in this index of thirty companies. Another criticism is that the strategy hasn't seemed to perform as well in recent years, which is true, though the kennel of dogs beat the Dow again in 2013. A third complaint argues that because the Dogs only advocates owning ten stocks, one stock can have an inordinate impact on the portfolio return. Also true, but not necessarily good or bad—it depends on the stock and the year. Some worry that the Dogs portfolio is equally weighted, which provides a performance advantage over the price-weighted DJIA. But, for those of us who are investing for future goals we are interested not necessarily in our performance relative to an index but in achieving our goals. We are more concerned about whether the strategy produces decent returns and the Dogs seems to do so. Not every year, but over time. The arbitrary re-balance date of January 1 worries other investors. Yet, if we are dollar-cost averaging with, say, our 401(k) contributions then we are also essentially selecting arbitrary investment dates, which seems to matter little. But, my favorite criticism is that these companies are unloved. Obviously. And that is the good news. We know that the best time to buy a great company is when it is unloved.

Each of the criticisms have some validity but each are mitigated by what history tells us about value stocks and particularly value stocks that pay a dividend. I am not advocating the Dogs of the Dow strategy. I don't employ the strategy myself though I own many of the stocks in the Dow. At the very least, the Dogs of the Dow or even the entire list of Dow Jones companies provides the value seeking investor with a great buy list to work from. But, the primary point is this: the simplicity of the strategy is appealing to those of us who are interested in achieving solid investment results without having to devote our entire life to doing so.

A Warning for Value Investors

Sometimes when a stock's yield is too high it is signaling bigger problems. It may be that the company has not encountered a temporary hitch but, in fact, the future looks exceedingly bleak. In that case investors will sell and push the price down and because dividend yield is also a ratio—dividend divided by price—when the price of the stock declines, the yield rises. Though a healthy yield provides valuation insight and a significant portion of our total return, a very high yield can signal danger. Competition from a new technology (think back to what digital photography did to Eastman Kodak's film business) or a severe earnings decline due to manufacturing or product liability issues can be nearly fatal for some companies and may result in a situation where the dividend is not sustainable and must be cut by management—a death knell for investors who are counting on the information provided through the dividend and who are depending on the yield for a portion of their total return. These are real worries for value investors.

Growth Versus Value Investing—a Summary

Value investors believe in reversion to the mean; that if they buy great companies at cheap valuations those stocks should outperform in the future. Conversely, growth investors are less concerned about the price of the stock than they are about the rate of sales or earnings growth. Growth investors know that if the earnings growth of a company is expected to exceed that of the average company then the stock price appreciation should accelerate as well. Note the operative word *should* in the assumptions made by both value and growth investors. As you are beginning to understand investing is less a science than an informed art. If we had to summarize one overriding characteristic of each style we might do so like this: value investors seek to purchase great, out-of-favor companies that are trading at depressed price levels with the hope that these great companies will fix their problems and the stock price will increase; growth investors seek to purchase technology and product disrupters whose long-term sustainable sales and earnings will grow in excess of the growth of the average company even if they have to pay a premium to get it.

Both styles—value and growth—can generate strong performance over the long-term but each style has positive and negative elements. Because the value investor is focused on price she is often buying into companies that have encountered a product or marketing problem, a slowing of earnings growth, or global economic headwinds—any organic or exogenous event that negatively impacts earnings and causes the price to decline. But,the beauty of buying value stocks is that she does not have to sustain exorbitant levels of volatility. Instead while waiting for management to right the earnings ship, she is often getting paid an upfront return via the dividend (which also aids in lowering volatility and dramatically enhancing total return). When the company does return to growth, a new constituent of investors (those interested in growth stocks) will become interested and potentially drive the price higher. As Peter Lynch has said, "The real key to making money in stocks is not to get scared out of them."

Suppose you find yourself with an investment temperament at neither extreme? Let's consider another approach—a hybrid approach, if you will—to value and growth investing, perhaps the most sensible strategy of all.

CHAPTER 5

Developing an Investment Discipline That Will Achieve Our Goals—Continued: The Stock Market Is a Tug-of-War between Fear and Greed; Arm Yourself with the Tools to Succeed

One of the first things every investor learns is not to take themselves too seriously. Arrogance is the first step down a slippery slope to potential portfolio losses. Just when we think we know all there is to know about a company a new technology is introduced and today's industry leader becomes yesterday's innovator. My colleagues and I used to call it the buggy-whip factor. No investor (or company management) wants to get caught making buggy-whips for a horse-drawn carriage on the eve of the invention of the automobile. Overconfidence or dependence on dogma too frequently results in unfortunate surprises. Because one of the most popular market investing dogmas is to assume the stock market is rational, pundits and researchers chant the maxim like a mantra. Yet I would argue (and behavioral economics seems to support me) that efficient markets exist only in theory. That people—who comprise the market—don't always make decisions based on rational, fact-based criteria. If we remember that the stock market is a tug-of-war between fear and greed, we will be much more likely to moderate our response to market swings. Any mother who has ever muttered the words, "My child would never do that" has likely come to regret the statement because inevitably her child does the very thing she decried. At least mine did—in spades. In my thirty years of investing, I have rarely observed the market to be rational. Especially at turning points. Yet that is exactly when the investor must herself be rational and consider the historical facts about stock market performance as well as underlying stock fundamentals and valuation when making investment decisions. By doing so she will not only reduce the odds of owning a buggy-whip company but will stay the course at turning points, which, after all, is how we make money.

In 1990 De Long et al. identified a class of investors whose enthusiasm for particular stocks—what they called investor sentiment—exceeded the stock's underlying fundamentals and caused prices to rise well above what those facts supported.[1] Investor sentiment works in the reverse as well, punishing stock prices well beyond the negative event would suggest. Yet, investors often choose to buy or not buy stocks based on their past (recent) performance, which implies they believe that past performance will continue. This assumption, while understandable, lacks the discipline we seek to apply as investors. If we keep in mind the tug-of-war, especially as buyers of attractively valued stocks, we will remember investors tend to overreact on the upside and downside. Knowing that provides us with the conviction required to follow our investment discipline at turning points. When I managed money for large institutions and families we were often presented with the opportunity to buy great growth stocks that had fallen from favor. And whenever we gathered to discuss one of the disgraced securities my colleague would say: "Well, it's either the warning bell or the dinner bell." And each time he said it, I would laugh, then consider the simple wisdom of his words. Because he was right. We were either onto something spectacular or a spectacular flop.

Buying growth stocks at a reasonable price (GARP) allows investors to whet both their growth and value appetites by buying highly regarded, growing companies at a value discount. If it is possible to achieve the best of both worlds then growth at a reasonable price exemplifies nirvana. It is here where we might see both Peter Lynch and Warren Buffett overlap—the intersection of growth and value investing. In fact, both legendary investors would tell you that they are interested in buying great companies with solid future growth prospects at a reasonable price—what we will refer to as Fallen Angel growth stocks.

As we discussed earlier the difference between traditional growth and value investing has a great deal to do with the investor's focus. While growth investors focus primarily on sales and earnings growth over stock price the opposite can generally be said about value investors. But, growth at a reasonable price investors can be much more agnostic about the style limitations of growth and value because their focus is not necessarily simply on sales or earnings growth nor is the focus only on price—GARP investors are interested in buying the best companies at reasonable prices. This criterion opens up the playing field.

A Few Words about Methods: How and When to Use the Price-to-Earnings Ratio as a Measure of Value

The dividend was the focus of our discussion of value stocks in the last chapter. I chose the dividend as our valuation tool because I spent twenty-plus years buying large value stocks employing the dividend as a primary indicator of value. We bucked the trend; most traditional value managers focus on the **price-to-earnings ratio (p/e)**, the most common valuation method considered and cited by investors seeking value.

The p/e is calculated simply by dividing the price per share of the stock by the earnings per share of the company. Most investors look at the p/e based on the trailing earnings of a company (TTM for trailing twelve months) because those numbers are the easiest to locate. The problem is that a p/e calculated based on TTM earnings only tells you how the stock is priced compared to the earnings it has produced in the past. Since the stock market is a forward-looking mechanism, the most important consideration is the stock's value or p/e based on expected future earnings. This is particularly true of the Fallen Angel whose price has presumably declined because the recent earnings have been a disappointment. (One of the best sites for estimated earnings and estimated p/e's is Bloomberg's public website. There you will find the p/e calculated based on both TTM earnings and future earnings as well as a comparison of the stock's p/e to the p/e of the S&P 500, a bell weather for the entire stock market. There you will also find the dividend yield for the stock as well as historical price charting capabilities, the date earnings are announced, and when the next dividend is paid. In short there is a plethora of financial data and news and charting options available for you to examine your Fallen Angel stock closely.) The forward p/e provides the investor with perspective on how much she is paying for a company's expected earnings. Since investors are really buying a portion of company earnings, when we buy a stock it is important to understand how much we are paying for those earnings. We can then comparison shop our company against other similar companies or against the entire market. Generally, when scouting for Fallen Angels we are looking for p/e's that are lower than the market p/e and lower than other stocks in the same industry.

Though I chose to employ the dividend as my primary valuation tool to identify cheap or value stocks in the previous chapter, the p/e is a common and useful tool for determining the value of a stock. I use it as a secondary indicator but many use it as the primary determinant of value. Often the p/e will confirm what the dividend tells me about the stock's attractiveness or provide me with conflicting information that may send me back to conduct more research. Remembering that the p/e is a ratio—the sum of two dynamic parts: the stock price and the company's earnings—is most useful in understanding how to use it as a tool.

A P/E EXAMPLE

You will hear references to the p/e frequently if you listen to or read financial news. The p/e is a standard of measure that most all investors understand. Growth stocks tend to carry high p/e's. Value stocks, low p/e's. The measure against which the high and low is judged is the p/e of the S&P 500, one of the broadest measures of the stock market. The average p/e ratio for the stocks that comprise the S&P 500 is historically around 15 times earnings. Let's assume for a moment I am interested in buying ABC stock, which trades at $100. But I am not sure if the stock is a bargain or overvalued. The earnings estimate for the next year is $7 per share. By dividing

$100 (the price of the stock) by $7 (the earnings estimate for the following year) I determine that the p/e ratio of ABC stock is 14.3x next year's earnings. The next measure to consider is how my 14.3x ratio compares to the p/e of the S&P 500. For the sake of argument let's assume the market is trading at its average p/e of 15x earnings. That means that ABC stock is cheaper than the market because I am paying somewhat less for a unit of future earnings. But it is not significantly cheaper enough than the market for me to be interested. I am looking for a discount of at least 25% to the p/e of the market. That's my measure. Yours may be more or less. But a 25% p/e discount hopefully limits my downside somewhat and allows for plenty of room on the upside. There are other factors to consider, of course. For example, maybe this stock always trades at a p/e discount so I want to look at history if possible. Maybe the forward earnings estimate does not appear to be obtainable based on the company's poor performance this year. If the earnings come in light then the stock price likely will deteriorate and my estimated p/e measure becomes meaningless. The p/e's value is considerable when earnings meet expectations. However, you may now better understand why the dividend paying culture of the company management becomes an important indicator. The management is providing us the best insight we will be able to glean about the company's future earnings prospects and with that information confirmed by the p/e as a secondary indicator we are bound to make better stock selection decisions.

FOR THE TRULY AMBITIOUS: THE PRICE/ EARNINGS-TO-GROWTH RATIO OR PEG

At the risk of wading a little too deep into the weeds, I want to introduce the concept of the PEG ratio. This measure adds one more dimension to the p/e ratio—the dynamic of earnings growth. The p/e tells me how much I am paying for earnings. The PEG tells me how much I am paying for earnings growth over an extended future period of time. Of course, the earnings growth is based on estimations but it is another benchmark of value. It takes the forward p/e to another level. A good rule of thumb is that a PEG below 1.0 is a good value indicator since it implies that I am paying less for future earnings growth; a PEG above the 1.0 level indicates the stock may be overvalued for the opposite reason. Of course, the accuracy of the earnings growth number will have an impact on the usefulness of the PEG as a valuation measure. We can calculate our own PEG using the earnings estimates published on Yahoo Finance or bloomberg.com or accept the shortcut offered by Bloomberg, which calculates the PEG ratio based on average estimated earnings.

The PEG is simply another input as we put together the puzzle of stock price valuation and selection.

How Do I Know a Fallen Angel Growth Stock When I See One?

Fallen Angels can best be characterized as yesterday's growth stock darling. In recent years stocks like Tiffany & Co., Coach Inc., Apple Computer, Coca Cola Company, Nordstrom Inc., Amgen, Inc. (biotech), Comcast Corp., Home Depot Inc., Walt Disney Company, McDonald's Corp., Nike Inc., Starbucks Corp., and Wal-Mart Stores, Inc. have fallen out of favor and reached attractive valuation levels. Some of these stocks may never return to growth stock status (though a good deal of money can be made in them nonetheless) but most will. As of the writing of this book one might argue that Tiffany, Disney, and Starbucks have returned to growth and their stock prices as measured by recent outperformance, yields, and p/e's would reflect that conclusion. The value buyer of these stocks has made a good deal of money as they have transitioned back to growth stock status. In chapter 1 we reviewed my purchase of Starbucks, a classic Fallen Angel. I became interested in the stock after it had declined 30 percent. I bought some and then it declined another approximately 70 percent because of factors specific to the company and factors related to the overall economic downturn. At that time I was busy with two teenagers and not exactly focused on my investment portfolio. Still it all worked out well enough in the end as it often does with quality companies. Despite the fact that I got in too early I've still enjoyed a healthy return in the stock.

So how do we identify Fallen Angels that are attractive for purchase? I hope you will forgive the shopping analogy; it feels like a tired old cliche but it's the best I can come up with. For the record, we already established in chapter 1 that I am not a shopper. Or at the very least not a very good bargain shopper. For me, shopping is a function of interest and time. I have rarely had either. Yet when it comes to stocks I am exceedingly keen on buying great companies on sale. Finding good-quality stocks selling for a discount involves the same effort, I imagine, as shopping for a bargain. If I go to the Nordstrom Rack in search of a new pair of designer shoes, I have to sort through shelves of boxes, hopping unsteadily on one foot while I search for the mate in the jumble of shoes piled on the floor. The search is time consuming and often frustrating. But if I persevere I often find a great value at a significantly lower price. At Nordstrom, the high-end department store, I am greeted warmly, offered a seat while the cheerful sales person schleps box after box for my consideration. He dutifully slips each shoe onto my foot, checking the length, the width, never tiring of helping me find just the right style and fit and color. And well he might because I am paying double or triple the price of shoes at the Rack. Of course the Rack shoes may be marred by a flaw but Rack shoppers expect this and, consequently, look the merchandise over carefully to determine if it is a flaw they can live with. This process is similar to buying shares in Fallen Angel growth stocks. More research and patience is required but when we get it right we enjoy growth stock returns at value prices.

Let's continue with an examination of Nordstrom (**stock ticker:** JWN), the stock, as an example of a classic Fallen Angel growth stock. Retailers live and die by the consumer. And just as one would expect, during the 2008–2009 downturn, Nordstrom stock, along with company sales, was punished. The stock declined from the mid-to-high 40s, bottoming around $10 per share. By the end of 2013, the stock was trading just shy of $62 per share but lagged the performance of the market and its primary competitor Macy's for the entire year. So the question savvy investors ask, is why Nordstrom, why now?

Returning to bloomberg.com to access the financial data we intend to examine we will begin with the dividend. We see that

JWN management has been growing the dividend by over 13 percent per year, about in line with earnings growth. The stock currently yields just under 2 percent. And though the management does not state an overt dividend policy (determined by a quick perusal of the company's annual report), their actions demonstrate a commitment to the dividend through a steady double-digit increase in line with earnings growth since initiating the payment of a dividend. The p/e seems to be trading at about the historical average rate for the stock, or in the 16–17x earnings range. Because earnings growth is expected to be flat from 2013 to 2104 the trailing and forward p/e are about the same and both are slightly below the p/e for the S&P 500. Not exactly conclusive. The PEG ratio is 1.4x, which would indicate we are paying a premium for future earnings growth. That premium leaves little room for error. So let's take a look at the p/s ratio that we introduced in the previous chapter as a measure of growth stock valuation. Nordstrom's p/s ratio is trading (like the p/e) in a normal historical range of around 1.0x. I happen to know—and you will, too, once you begin compiling information on the stocks you are interested in—that JWN's p/s ratio has been as high as 1.8x before the recession and as low as 0.25x at the stock's trough. So what we glean from the p/s ratio is consistent with the p/e: the stock seems to be fairly valued. The PEG would argue that the stock is somewhat overvalued, yet the dividend growth signals that management is satisfied with expectations of 12–13% long-term earnings growth. Now what?

We clearly need to do more research. An excellent site for women investors who seek insightful analysis and financial information on stocks is *Seeking Alpha*. By registering as a user you will receive email alerts whenever there is news on stocks you are following. The site is a rich resource of the "story" surrounding a stock's performance. Earnings reports and updates are available along with opinion pieces posted by regular contributors. I read the posts on a handful of stocks where I lack detailed knowledge and focus on the factual content presented rather than the opinions. I rarely take advice from people whose track record is unknown to me. The same should hold true for you.

*A **digression**: I have referenced an appendix (located in the back of this book) with a list of free websites like Seeking Alpha that can shortcut your research process significantly. I will rarely tell you to seek the consensus or mainstream opinion but one very reliable source—especially as we consider the Fallen Angel—is Barron's. This weekly print and digital publication, among other things, offers the best ideas of their journalists (who are more like practitioners, providing in-depth analysis and a record of the results of their recommendations). Barron's also features the ideas of some of the best money managers in the country, or world, for that matter. By reading faithfully you will eventually understand which journalist or columnist offers stock ideas that complement your investing strategy and temperament, and which featured money managers do the same. The publication has been an invaluable tool for me over the years (especially in the "examining for defects" part of my research) and presents ideas in a manner that is accessible to any investor: novice or expert. Because the weekly is available digitally you can access whatever you want whenever you want. Stories are updated in real time; the data is rich and comprehensive. All for $100 per year. I've paid for my subscription ten times over with just one good idea.*

So what I learn in summary from reading the research and news on Nordstrom is that the company is investing in e-commerce and an expansion plan into Canada, which has had a dampening effect on earnings growth. And, though JWN is a high-end retailer, the company is growing the discount Nordstrom Rack and expects 50 percent of future growth to come from the Rack. Canadian expansion, e-commerce, and the opening of a flagship store in New York City bode well for future earnings growth. The financial ratios tell me that the company, for the most part, seems to be fairly priced. Neither a compelling value, nor particularly over-priced. We could wait for a better (lower) entry point or we may decide to initiate a small position expecting that the stock will appreciate in line with earnings (and dividend) growth of approximately 12–13 percent—a healthy return. By doing the research, we have removed the impact of emotion and increased our confidence no matter which choice we make. And, after thirty years of investing I do know that I have never been sorry to wait for a lower entry point. Not once.

A WARNING FOR GARP INVESTOR WHEN IT COMES TO FALLEN ANGELS

This is a good place to discuss the most difficult aspect of investing in Fallen Angels: timing. A little patient foot-dragging when buying Fallen Angels has rarely cost me money; getting in the way of sellers running for the exits has. Wait for the dust to settle. Remember that prior to stumbling, Fallen Angels were owned by growth investors who are rarely patient with earnings misses and often unload a stock at the first sign of weakness; they can and will bail out of a stock much quicker than the more price-sensitive investor can or should accumulate holdings. Watch. Wait. The former darling will pass through the three stages of stock market grief: disappointment, hate, and finally, neglect. Neglect is the point where the stock price flatlines: the optimal place to begin buying.

I once had a client ask me: "If you know a stock is going to decline further why don't you just wait?" After an initial suppressed and smug giggle—for how would I know precisely when it was done declining?—I realized the simple brilliance behind his question. Why not wait? Being first when buying Fallen Angels is not the point. The worse that can happen if one chooses to wait is that you miss an opportunity to own a great growth company. What is more likely to happen is that you may ride the stock down further and truncate your total return (my Starbucks example). I have solved this in my own portfolio by establishing a price target where I will consider purchasing a Fallen Angel. I may still be early but I've limited my potential losses by predetermining just how early I will begin buying the stock.

Intelligent Investing Rule #5: *The stock market is a tug-of-war between fear and greed. Buying from fearful sellers and selling to greedy buyers is optimal. But the savvy woman will require more* *than just good instincts to do so. Develop your discipline, employ the valuation tools we've discussed, and do your research.*

The beauty of buying growth stocks at a reasonable price is that we do not have to sustain exorbitant levels of volatility as we might when buying pure growth stocks. Instead while waiting for management to right the earnings ship, we are often getting paid an upfront return via the dividend (which also aids in lowering volatility) to sit tight. When the company does return to growth, a new constituent of investors (those focused on growth stocks) will become interested and drive the price higher. As Peter Lynch has said, "The real key to making money in stocks is not to get scared out of them" and by informing ourselves we can develop the confidence required to hold our ground at turning points. And not get "scared out."

But, perhaps, the soundest advice comes from the "First Woman of Finance," Muriel Siebert who said, "You make money by taking a stand and being right." If your research and discipline is sound (and it will be) better to ask yourself during times of price weakness not, "Should I be selling?" but "Should I be buying more?"

WHATEVER WE CALL IT, SUCCESSFUL INVESTORS BUY GREAT COMPANIES THAT FOR THE MOST PART WILL CONTINUE TO PRODUCE SOLID LONG-TERM PERFORMANCE

Though I might have cited Warren Buffett as the quintessential value investor, that is not necessarily how he sees himself. In 2000 Buffett wrote in his annual shareholder's letter: "Market commentators and investment managers who glibly refer to 'growth' and 'value' styles as contrasting approaches to investment are displaying their ignorance, not their sophistication. Growth is simply a component [usually a plus, sometimes a minus] in the value equation." Peter Lynch would likely argue a similar view since it is he who is also credited with popularizing the GARP style of investing. In both cases, these legendary investors are buying the best companies at the most attractive prices. And the best companies by definition have strong management teams. Whether you decide to buy traditionally characterized growth stocks or value stocks or growth stocks at a reasonable price, when you buy the stocks of great companies you can count on the fact the company management is doing the heavy lifting. Buffett's characterization of the "value equation" is the right place to focus. Price is one of the variables investors can and should control.

Exchange-Traded Funds (ETFs), The Antidote for Women Who Do Not Have the Time Nor the Interest to Buy Individual Stocks

By all accounts the first and still largest ETF, the SPDR (which traces the S&P 500 and is referred to as the "Spider") was launched by State Street Global Advisors in 1993. There were a few earlier funds but State Street's was the first commercially viable launch and remains the largest ETF today, with $58 billion in assets accounting for sixteen or so percent of all ETF assets. Interestingly though it was Pattie Dunn, the first woman to serve as CEO of a large investment management company in the United States who is responsible for creating the first ETFs franchise—the iShares. As CEO of Barclays Global Investors (formerly Wells Fargo Investment Advisors) Dunn, in 1996, took the industry lead launching the iShares family of ETFs. She is credited with providing the vision, leadership, and marketing savvy that grew the iShares franchise to dominate the industry by the time it was sold to BlackRock in 2009 for $13.5 billion. From secretary to CEO, Pattie Dunn played a lead role in creating a trillion dollar industry that suits today's women investors in many ways. As we will see.

First, a quick primer on ETFs and what they are and are not. ETFs originated in the 1980s but have grown enormously over the last decade, now boasting over $1 trillion in assets invested in the funds. They continue to grow at an astounding rate while mutual fund growth languishes in the mid-single digits. ETFs are funds— funds of stocks replicating a specific index—that trade like stocks. Which is to say they trade in and are priced in real time. These funds replicate particular indexes like the S&P 500, the largest stocks in the NASDAQ, dividend paying stocks, dividend growth stocks, or growth stocks. They focus on industries like health care, financial institutions, retailers, oil companies, consumer discretionary, or industrials. Further delineations can be found in small- or mid-capitalization stocks or international or country-specific stocks. Bond indexes are also replicated by ETFs. New funds pop up monthly and the ETF can be as focused or broad as their portfolio objective dictates. ETFs provide us with an opportunity to diversify our investment portfolio into areas where we lack expertise. I own ETFs that replicate small- and mid-cap stocks, and international stocks to name a few. Sometimes if I want some exposure to a particular group, I will buy an ETF. Particularly if I don't have time to conduct the kind of research I demand for an individual holding. ETFs increase our flexibility and our reach. But one of the most important characteristics of ETFs (and particularly as they relate to mutual funds) is their low fees.

Low ETF Fund Fees Contribute Significantly to Long-Term Performance

Investment management fees are the single greatest risk to long-term investment performance. According to Morningstar, the average actively managed stock mutual fund sports an annual expense ratio of over 1.4 percent. Compare this to the average ETF fee of 0.20 percent. Let's assume your portfolio returns in line with the long-term average annual stock market return of approximately 9 percent. And let's further assume the average inflation rate (since 1913) of approximately 3 percent per year. This leaves a real return of 6 percent on your portfolio. Before fees. Add in the average annual expense ratio of 1.4 percent, and you are left with a total return of 4.6 percent. The mutual fund management fee in one year alone costs almost 23 percent of your real total return versus a cost of 3.3 percent of your real total return if you were invested in an ETF with an average fee of 0.20 percent. But now let's look at the impact of fees over the long-term. To do so we will turn to a study conducted by the US Department of Labor (DOL).

The DOL has published an interesting analysis of the eroding effects of 401(k) fees on long-term investor returns (available on their website and summarized here). The study first considers an individual with a 401(k) balance of $25,000 who has 35 years remaining until retirement and who pays an investment management fee of 0.5 percent (a conservative assumption) and earns 7 percent per year (a reasonable assumption). At the end of the 35-year period and assuming no additional contributions (unlikely and, therefore, conservative), the balance will grow to $277,000. However, increase the fee to 1.5 percent (somewhat aggressive), and keep all of the other assumptions the same and the account balance grows to only $163,000—or $114,000 less than the portfolio paying the lower fee. According to the DOL, that 1 percent higher fee compounded over 35 years reduces the ultimate account balance by 28 percent. The negative power of compounding an excessive fee. Yet that fee is closer to the average many people pay in their 401(k) account. The benefit of owning ETFs with significantly lower fees is obvious.

But the erosive effect actually runs much deeper than the simple calculation above. Let's consider a 2013 paper by William F. Sharpe, professor emeritus of finance at Stanford University and 1990 winner of the Nobel Prize in Economic Sciences entitled, "The Arithmetic of Investment Expenses."[2] The article was published in the *Financial Analysts Journal* and argues, "a person saving for retirement who chooses low-cost investments could have a standard of living throughout retirement more than 20% higher than that of a comparable investor in high-cost investments." The impact of fees, especially over the long-term is profound. Sharpe cites two important statistics in the opening paragraphs. The first comes from Charles Ellis' 2012 paper "Investment Management Fees Are (Much) Higher Than You Think." Ellis points out that while investors may consider the investment management fee being levied against their total assets as relatively minor, the true measure is how large those fees loom against the actual incremental returns generated by the manager.[3] For example, you hand over a $50,000 retirement account to a mutual fund with an expense ratio of 1.4 percent ($700 annual fee calculated on the invested amount of $50,000) and are thrilled with a gain of $10,000 or 20 percent in one year though the market performs about the same. But when considered against the backdrop of the fee paid to gain that $10,000, it is easy to see that you paid perhaps much more than you considered. You earned and saved and provided the fund manager with the $50,000 investment. His fee to produce the $10,000 gain is roughly $700 in the first year. Or 7 percent. Which means your net gain is actually 13 percent in a year when the market returned 20 percent. And the analysis becomes even bleaker when considered against how much your portfolio would have returned if you had simply invested it in a passive ETF, say one that emulates the S&P 500 and charges 0.05 percent compared to the average 1.4 percent mutual fund fee. Looked at it in this context, investment management fees are exorbitant. And then some.

But perhaps the most damning statistic Sharpe cites is from a 2010 paper published by Russel Kinnel in the *Morningstar FundInvestor.* Kinnel is the director of fund research at Morningstar, the leading provider of mutual fund analysis and he writes and Sharpe quotes: "If there's anything in the whole world of mutual funds that you can take to the bank, it's that expense ratios help you make a better decision. In every single time period and data point tested, low-cost funds beat high-cost funds."[4] High fees are one of the most dependable (and erosive) predictors of underperformance.

The impact of fees on total return is surely significant and though not necessarily the subject of this chapter, is a topic we will return to. What is important for our purposes here is to understand that ETFs provide a low-cost alternative to mutual funds. From the research it would appear that while an individual mutual fund may provide sound performance, after fees are paid investors accumulate comparatively more wealth in lower cost (even if they might be lower performing) alternatives.

ETFs Pricing Is Easy to Access, Which Makes the Funds Easy to Trade

Mutual funds are priced at the close of each trading day, which means that investors allocating money to a particular mutual fund are essentially investing in the fund without knowing the closing price they will be paying for their shares. Since orders are often placed during trading hours and funds are not priced until the close of the market investors lose flexibility or, at the very least, they lose the ability to control the one thing we have asserted is the most important thing to control when investing: the price. ETFs on the other hand trade like a stock. The price is offered in real time and I know at any second of the trading day the value of my holdings or the price I will be paying for my shares. ETFs provide the investor with the flexibility to opportunistically invest. For our purposes as long-term investors, we are not necessarily too concerned about short-term pricing, but on principle, I like to know what I am paying for any given investment I choose to make. I can buy and sell an ETF any time during the trading day. I know precisely what I am paying for the ETF because the funds, like stocks, are priced in real time. I am controlling the variable I can control. Price. As the great Jack Bogle, founder of Vanguard Group and the king of passive, low-cost investing, once said about investing, "The only thing that works with any consistency is low cost."

ETFs Are Tax Efficient

Now here is where it gets a little tricky.

ETFs are more tax efficient than mutual funds. ETF investors incur potential taxable gains or losses when they sell their holdings—just like a stock. Not so with mutual fund holdings. As a shareholder in a mutual fund you participate in the fund on a pro-rata basis with all the other mutual shareholders. Think of the homeowners association of a condo complex. Everyone shares in the expenses together. If the roof over Unit 4C is leaking, the collective funds of the community pay for the repair. If a mutual fund manager takes capital gains, each shareholder reaps their corresponding portion of the tax liability for the capital gains. Those gains or losses are typically calculated after the October 31 fiscal year end most funds observe. As an investor you are unable to plan for potential gains or losses or capital distributions made by the fund, creating a potentially unknown tax liability. Worse, there are times when mutual funds are forced to distribute capital gains (thereby creating a tax liability for the shareholder) although the fund has delivered a negative performance for the year. This happened in 2001 when the market sold off after the terrorist attacks on 9/11 and investors fled the market and their mutual funds. Managers were forced to sell stocks to raise cash for those exiting the funds and often were forced to sell holdings where they had long-term capital gains. Most funds posted a negative return for the year yet their shareholders still had to pay capital gains tax. It is a little like being ambushed. You can't plan if you don't know. But, this problem does not occur with ETFs as the funds accommodate investment flows by creating or redeeming a separate pool of assets called "creation units." As an investor, you rarely incur a taxable event until you decide to sell your holdings. In other words, you are in control of your tax liability.

ETFs Increase Your Ability to Diversify Your Portfolio; an Added Benefit? Investors Are Less Likely to Fall in Love With an ETF Than a Stock

If left to my own biases I would construct my portfolio entirely of large-cap, US companies that pay a dividend. Those are the stocks I feel comfortable with; they represent the segment I know and understand. But a portfolio with that kind of concentration is not prudent. What about smaller companies? Or international companies? What about bonds, for that matter? Or an industry segment where I am not particularly savvy or just don't have the conviction to select stocks? ETFs fill in the gap. They allow investors (again!) the ultimate flexibility to gain exposure to a particular group at a low cost and with complete control over when and how much they will pay for that exposure. In chapter 11, I share a collection of ETFs to own for a lifetime. Still you will want to do your own research. Funds that emulate the S&P 500 can be had almost anywhere for an annual fee of approximately 0.05 percent or lower. But specialty funds can charge well above the 0.20 percent average. Be discriminating. And cost-focused. The most expensive ETF fee I pay is 0.20 percent. I cannot fathom a reason for you to pay more.

If you are busy (and who isn't) or you are worried about your ability to select and pay attention to individual stock holdings,

ETFs are a great place to start. You can build a diversified and cost-controlled portfolio with modest effort. Additionally, there are extensive resources available on the Internet to allow you the ability to compare fees and fund offerings. The low-cost providers: Vanguard, Schwab, and iShares dominate the industry but there are many interesting fund offerings that may captivate you. For example, I own the PowerShares QQQ, which seeks to emulate the NASDAQ 100 Index for a fee of 0.20 percent. Although I own some of the stocks also held in the QQQ's I can monitor the fund holdings by going to the PowerShares website. In this way I can ensure I know where the overlap exists and manage my stock holdings accordingly. And as my holdings in the QQQ's appreciate and I begin trimming them (we will be discussing portfolio construction in chapter 6) I find I am much less likely to fall in love with an ETF than a stock I have owned for awhile. For some reason we have the potential to become emotionally attached to stocks in a way we don't with a fund. I recently had the opportunity to sell my Tiffany holdings. I acquired the Fallen Angel a few years ago and the stock has appreciated back to growth stock levels. I sold all but 100 shares. I just couldn't sell it all. It's a shame to admit but I love receiving the robin's egg blue annual report each year.

A WARNING ABOUT ETFs

The biggest downside to ETFs is their potential volatility. Because they emulate an index, the funds will rise and fall with the particular market segment they represent. When we buy value stocks our portfolios will assuredly decline in a market downturn but will likely decline less. Value stocks (and this includes growth stocks at a reasonable price) have two advantages in down markets. The first is that the price of the stock has already underperformed in order for the stock to become interesting to value investors and, therefore, presumably has less downside risk than the high-fliers. The second advantage is the dividend. This portion of the total return is more or less guaranteed and provides a further cushion in declining markets. ETFs will rise and fall with the same magnitude as the index they represent. Over the long-term your ETF investments will do well but in the short-term they may experience more price volatility.

If up to me, I would advise you to focus on three of the styles we have discussed in the last two chapters. We learned that value outperforms growth over the long-term in all capitalization ranges and in almost every market around the globe. We also learned that growth investing is not for the faint of heart nor for those women who are short on time. We discovered a relatively easy way to invest in value stocks by buying large companies with significant and sound dividend payment policies or constructing a portfolio following the Dogs of the Dow theory, and we examined the potential to own growth stocks at a reasonable price, which is simply another way of searching for value. We also discovered how accessible financial research and data is for those of us on the run. Free websites contain data I used to pay tens of thousands of dollars for annually as a professional investor and are now available to anyone with a smart phone or a mouse. And finally, in our quest to understand the benefits of ETFs we also discovered the importance of low fees on the accumulation of wealth and how to gain exposure to specific industries, countries or capitalization ranges. Before we dig into some actual stock case studies let's take a look at how to construct a portfolio. And why it matters.

CHAPTER 6

Construct Your Portfolio Like a Dinner Party Invitation List: Holdings Should Be Balanced and Behave Well If Things Get Out of Hand

If you've ever been held hostage to an obnoxious seatmate during a dinner party you understand the value of a well-thought-out invitation and seating plan. The companion who talks too much, drinks too much, or displays bad table manners can turn an enjoyable evening out into an ordeal. A good hostess knows this and will create an invitation and seating list that complements each guest's interests or vocation. Because when the conversation and camaraderie are humming, the party is a success.

Such is the case with your portfolio. How we weight the particular stock holdings or ETFs we select will have a profound impact not only on our total return but also on the levels of volatility we experience. Here again, plenty of research has been conducted on the question of portfolio construction. Let's take a quick look at one of the landmark studies penned by Brinson, Hood, and Beebower. Their original work "Determinants of Portfolio Performance" was published in 1986. A follow-up study published in the January–February 1995 issue of the *Financial Analysts Journal* under the same name is the focus of our analysis.[1] Brinson et al. studied the results of 91 large pension plans from 1974 to 1983. And what they found is encouraging for women who are interested in managing our own portfolios. In effect, the results show that professional management detracts from total return. This should provide us with additional confidence that successful investing is more about establishing our future family goals, developing an investment strategy designed to meet those goals, and having the courage and discipline to leave those investments alone until we need to access the funds.

THE IMPACT OF ASSET ALLOCATION AND SECURITY SELECTION ON INVESTMENT RETURNS; OR WHY BUSY WOMEN CAN FEEL CONFIDENT IN THEIR ABILITY TO INVEST

Brinson established four quadrants of measurement. Quadrant I represented the return produced by the established asset allocation policy. (We were introduced to asset allocation policy in chapter 3.) Quadrant II measured the return effects of the fund manager's deviation from the policy. Quadrant III measured the performance attributed to how well the manager selected stocks and bonds. Quadrant IV considered the total return of the total fund over the entire period. In other words, the sum total of all the elements examined in the other three quadrants.

The best level of performance was 10.11 percent achieved by the quadrant I performance, which sought to measure the impact of asset allocation alone (calculated based on the performance of the relevant index in each asset class). The kind of return we might experience if we chose to build a portfolio using ETFs that track the indices. What Brinson's work showed was the more inputs the fund manager added, the lower the portfolio return. Simply establishing a portfolio based on a fixed asset allocation, investing the money in the corresponding indices, and leaving it alone generated the highest level of performance. The simplest, least complicated strategy performed the best.

This should encourage each of us. And should reinforce what we've learned about why women make better investors than men. We have the natural instinct to set the course and leave it alone. No tweaking or tampering—we are far too busy for that. For the most part we just set our policy and allow it to play out. When my husband and I were first married I worked very hard at trying to make sure we sat down to dinner. We both worked long hours so the activity was definitely a joint effort. We divided duties and I happily left him alone to execute his. But, eventually I realized that while I was letting the pot simmer he was adding ingredients to my dishes and what ended up on the table bore little resemblance to the recipe I intended to prepare. He added ketchup to the beef stroganoff, water to the chilli, salt to the already salty marinade, too much cayenne to the jambalaya. He couldn't seem to help himself. He wanted to add his own signature to the meal while I was content to implement the recipe as written. Occasionally he hit on a winning combination but more often than not we agreed we liked the original dish better. Just as Brinson showed that setting an asset allocation policy and leaving it alone generated the best return, we found that following the spirit of the recipe (read: no ketchup in the stroganoff) produced the best meals. This is not to say we didn't, over time, add a little more of one spice while cutting back on another, or substitute healthier ingredients when it suited the overall dish, because we did. As with cooking when we invest we don't simply stick with our asset allocation policy forever and let our investments ride. Particularly when our goals change, or in the case of food—our taste buds. We make informed adjustments; proactive choices versus reactive ones. As some of our investments appreciate we trim them back to match our policy and as others underperform we consider adding to them. We may choose to do this quarterly or annually, whenever suits. But the trick is to be consistent. Just as pruning a rosebush results in healthier blooms, the same is true for our overall portfolio.

There is no doubt women are busy. And busy mastering a dozen different tasks. Still, we seem to be made for juggling multiple ideas and tasks. *The Wall Street Journal* reported in December of 2013 on the differences in "brain wiring" between young men and women.[2] The trailblazing research was directed by neurologist Neda Jahanshad, of the University of Southern California while she worked at the University of California at Los Angeles. The results have created a stir in the neurological community, leading one researcher to refer to them as "incendiary": women's and men's brains are wired differently. The results show that women demonstrate more connections *between* their left and right hemispheres while men seem to be better connected *within* hemispheres. The conclusion? The research results suggest that women are likely better at multitasking and analytical thought requiring coordination between the left and right brain. While I did not necessarily require science to confirm what I've repeatedly experienced, the study results should give women further confidence to trust our ability to analyze and multitask—important components of a successful investor.

A Real-Life Portfolio Left to Its Own Devices

Over ten years ago I gave an interview to a publication called *The Wall Street Transcript*. I came across it quite by accident one night as I was researching stocks on the Internet. Of course, I read with great interest the stocks I had recommended a decade prior. Particularly since that ten-year period has been a difficult time for investors. In the article I recommended five stocks from different industries. Each of the five I considered to be high-quality, industry leaders with strong management teams; each out of favor for some reason. The five stocks I discussed in April of 2003 were Genentech (**stock ticker:** DNA, purchased by Roche Holdings in 2009), Cisco Systems (**stock ticker:** CSCO), The Walt Disney Company (**stock ticker:** DIS), Citigroup (**stock ticker:** C), and General Electric (**stock ticker:** GE). Table 6.1 calculates the performance of each stock on a weekly compounded basis from the close of trading on April 11, 2003 (the last trading day before the article was published on April 14) through April 12, 2013. The first number shown is the absolute and cumulative return of the stock during the entire

Table 6.1 Five stock portfolio returns, April 11, 2003–April 12, 2013

Stock	Cumulative performance	Annualized performance
Genentech	432.9%	32.5%
Cisco	70.8%	5.2%
Disney	350.6%	14.5%
Citigroup	−84.8%	−17.2%
General Electric	20.1%	1.8%
Portfolio return	**249.7%**	**9.6%**
S&P 500	109.4%	7.7%

period. The second number is the average annual return for each of the ten years. To obtain a total portfolio return I assumed all five stocks were equally weighted.

You can see that the portfolio outperformed the market but this example demonstrates how important diversification is to achieving total return. Only two of the five stocks dramatically outperformed the market over the period, one came close to matching the market, and two underperformed. One of those stocks not only underperformed but generated a significantly negative return. But in spite of that the portfolio as a whole outperformed the market by 2 percent per year for the ten years measured. What can we conclude from the performance of these stocks? Three things. First, diversification is always important. Despite making sound, thoughtful investment decisions we cannot possibly know which stock will quadruple and which one will tank. But we can make sure we spread our risk exposure; the diversification offered by this five-stock portfolio is not simply among different companies but companies within different economic sectors and industries: biotech, technology, entertainment, banking, and industrials. The second thing we learn is that we can have one or two laggards and still do as well as or better than the market overall. And, lastly, we can conclude that over time, well-managed companies generally find ways to overcome adversity and generate strong returns.

What is the optimal level of diversification? Many years ago, Peter L. Bernstein, founder of the *Journal of Portfolio Management,* wrote, "Diversification is the only rational deployment of our ignorance." There are times when, despite our best research efforts, our stocks or ETFs are affected by external events beyond our control. If you had asked me over ten years ago which of those five stocks I believed would underperform the most dramatically I would not have been able to identify Citigroup (which, interestingly, was featured in *Barron's* in December 2013 as one of their top ten stocks for 2014). Conversely, I also would have been unable with any certainty to pick Genentech as the top performer. I believed, based on my research, that each of those five stocks had the *potential* to outperform, which is why we own more than one stock.

So is there an optimal level of diversification? And if so, what is it?

DIVERSIFICATION, IT WOULD SEEM, IS IN THE EYE OF THE BEHOLDER

We could comb the entirety of the research on the question of optimal portfolio diversification and come up with a variety of answers. Let's begin by approaching the subject from the perspective of our dinner party invitation list. One of the first factors that will enter into the decision of how many people to invite to our dinner party is the size of the table. If your dining table is small you will compile a small invitation list. The same will be true of your portfolio. If your assets are modest you will likely select an ETF with broad market exposure or invest in a few **blue-chip stocks** with either a pure value or GARP valuation. As your assets grow you will become more interested in increasing the number and breadth of your holdings. Just as your dinner party invitation list will be determined by the capacity.

Once the number of potential guests is determined the next question becomes whom to invite. And here is where the art enters in. You may choose your guest list considering people who share common interests like running or politics or religion or maybe because your kids play sports together. Yet you would probably won't invite someone you know will clash with your other guests. The purpose of considering your guest list carefully is to ensure a harmonious and enjoyable evening. The same is true for your portfolio. You want to build a list of holdings that complement each other. You would not select all your stocks from the same industry because generally speaking they will all perform similarly during various economic cycles. Better to select the top company—the industry leader or market share dominator—if you are buying individual stocks or an ETF that tracks the industry. And as you gain sophistication you will begin to understand that some industries do well when others don't. We call this **correlation**. A well-constructed portfolio will own securities from various industries that enjoy low levels or negative levels of correlation so that the portfolio return will be smoother than it would be with a severe concentration in one area.

Back to the dinner party. Many years ago our group of friends met monthly for dinner. Inevitably I was seated next to the same man and inevitably he drank too much before we had even reached the table. One night he spilled a glass of red wine on the hostess' antique embroidered tablecloth. The guests sped into action. Someone suggested club soda. Another ran next door to grab her supply. Still someone else put on a pot of coffee. And a wise fellow grabbed our wayward friend and walked him around the block. The rest of us went to work on the tablecloth and the combination of the club soda and teamwork restored the prized antique. Though we ended up eating with our plates on our laps in the living room, the party was salvaged. The diversity and individual talents of the guests eventually produced a harmonious evening despite the external event that set the evening off course. Undoubtedly our host did not anticipate the calamity but her guest list was comprised of people who worked well together. The evening was the better for it. You will find the same benefits when you carefully construct your portfolio.

GUIDELINES FOR CONSTRUCTING A PORTFOLIO OF US STOCKS

There are many rules of thumb. But, I have found that owning fewer stocks is simpler and easier for me to research thoroughly. When I was managing money for large institutions I discovered a study by Morningstar Principia Pro (long ago misplaced) that measured the returns of mutual funds over a ten-year period based on the number of stocks owned. The categories ranged from 10–20 stocks to over 100 stocks. Surprisingly, the best performing segment—by an average of 2–3 percent per year—was the most concentrated category: mutual funds that held between 10 and 20 stocks (14 stocks on average). This segment was also the only category that beat the market. And it did so by just under 2 percent per year. Every other category underperformed the market over the ten-year period. The reason for this? When managers over-diversify it is difficult for them to beat a broad market index because their portfolio begins looking too much like the index. And this is especially true—as we all know—after the fee is deducted. I've noticed that the results are the same for my own portfolios. The smaller ones own between 10 and 12 stocks and almost always outperform the larger portfolios with 20–30 holdings.

The first thing I do when building a portfolio is take a look at the **economic sector** weightings in the S&P 500. Sectors are comprised of industries that make up that particular economic sector. This exercise is easy to effect. I go to the S&P Dow Jones Index website published by McGraw Hill Financial and click on S&P 500 and then Sector Breakdown. (The website address is listed in the appendix.) In this way I am able to view the sector weightings on any given day. And though the weightings fluctuate (as the stocks in a particular sector appreciate, its weighting rises relative to the other sectors) the relative weightings are consistent enough over time to provide a valuable guideline. Table 6.2 shows the weightings as of early December 2013.

What I am interested in is not letting my portfolio get too far out of whack with the market. By that I mean I don't want my holdings in, say, the consumer discretionary sector to represent more than a 50 percent premium to the 12.5 percent the sector represents of the total market. The reason I sold my Tiffany stock was not only because the stock had almost doubled over the previous two years, but because it appreciated, my weighting in the

Table 6.2 S&P 500 sector weightings, December 6, 2013

S&P 500 sector	Percent weighting
Information technology	18.1
Financials	16.2
Health care	13.2
Consumer discretionary	12.5
Industrials	10.8
Energy	10.4
Consumer staples	10.0
Materials	3.4
Utilities	3.0
Telecommunication services	2.4

consumer discretionary sector had risen above my targeted guideline. When my sector weightings appreciate above my allotted 50 percent premium to the S&P sector weighting I have learned I may be taking an unintended risk. Stock market researchers watch these weightings to track areas where the market may be overvalued. Bespoke Investment Group regularly publishes commentary on the performance of the S&P sectors. Their research covers historical analysis of these sectors to provide a broader understanding of US economic performance and to provide indications of when a sector is becoming overvalued. For example, technology currently represents about 18 percent of the S&P but right before the dotcom bubble burst, technology represented well over 30 percent of the S&P, up from 5 percent only ten years prior. Although we are long-term investors we still gain valuable insight from tracking the sector weightings. But most important is that we don't allow our holdings to appreciate above our specified guidelines. My rule (as mentioned) is not to allow a sector to appreciate over 50 percent more than the S&P sector weighting. When my holdings in consumer discretionary stocks rose to 18 percent of my portfolio (and the sector represented 12.5 percent in the S&P 500) I trimmed the most expensive stocks in the sector (starting with Tiffany). Knowing if a sector is under- or over-weighted in the S&P based on historical levels provides valuable information regarding which underlying stocks or ETFs we may want to add to our portfolio. Or which ones we may want to trim back. But before you feel overwhelmed, recall Brinson's research. Establishing our strategy and implementing it without fuss provides enviable returns. Additional knowledge can add value but, most importantly, provides us with the courage to stick to our strategy.

It is helpful to also note the individual industries within a particular sector. It is not necessary to own securities in each industry. We mostly want to know which sector they fall into. And the information is easy to access. Recently I researched under the term: *Industries in the Consumer Discretionary sector* and found a great listing on the Fidelity Research website. Some of the industries within the Consumer Discretionary sector are: autos, hotels and leisure, household durables, Internet and catalog retail, media, multiline and specialty retail, as well as textiles, apparel, and luxury goods to name a few. Companies like Disney, Nike, Tiffany, Coach, Nordstrom, Macy's Under Armor, Amazon, and Michael Kors are leaders in their respective industry within the Consumer Discretionary sector and may form a list of companies you are interested in researching.

Remember, focus on the leaders with good management teams, market share dominance that improves pricing power and ultimately earnings, and attractive valuations. To get to know a company, I make a file and put clippings or research I've uncovered about the stock. And, I examine the ratios we discussed in the previous chapters. In this way I compile my list and ultimately my portfolio. Efficiently, deliberately, much the same way we manage most activities in our lives.

Portfolio Construction to Meet Our Financial Goals Depends a Good Deal on Our Time Horizon

We will be considering two different kinds of portfolios: one allocated entirely to ETFs and then a portfolio mix of stocks and ETFs. It is possible, of course, to build a portfolio entirely of individual securities in all capitalization sizes but doing so effectively is simply a function of the time available to you to conduct research. If you are as busy as I think you are you will find one of my two examples, at the very least, a good starting point. But first, a brief digression.

For those of you who are just embarking on your career or in the early stages of building a family, you have the luxury of time for your assets to grow to meet your future financial objectives. If you completed the exercise in the earlier chapter on goals-based investing you may have established (either literally or through mental accounting) at least three different accounts: an education account, a retirement account, and a wealth accumulation or savings account. In that same chapter we saw the asset allocation policies suggested by our three experts for various stages of achieving our financial goals. The allocations were heavily weighted toward stocks even as the life event drew closer.

I once had the opportunity to manage money for a descendant of the founder of one of the country's venerable bond houses. He was in his eighties when we first met to discuss his portfolio. I expected his portfolio to be filled with bonds—after all his family wealth came from selling bonds to other wealthy families and institutions and he was getting up there. Instead, what I found was an aggressively oriented portfolio comprised entirely of growth stocks, a portfolio chockablock full of growth stocks for this eighty-something purveyor of fixed income securities. In response to what I had hoped was an imperceptible raising of the brows he chuckled and said, "I view my investing time horizon as infinity." His wealth was for his heirs and their time horizon was much longer, presumably, than his. Therefore, he maintained an aggressive allocation, even though the actuarial tables might argue otherwise. As for the lack of bonds—and I am paraphrasing here—he mumbled something like: you can't make any real money in bonds.

I am not debating the value of bonds. They certainly have their place in a portfolio. And, of course, there are times you can make money owning bonds. At the end of 2013 the Federal Reserve announced they will begin the tapering of the behemoth easing program that has fueled the extended bond rally and kept bond rates unnaturally low. (It is certainly true that the "easy" Fed policy has also benefited stocks but our focus here is bonds.) Expectations are that bond rates will rise in the ensuing years. If so, bond prices will decline. (Remember that bond yields are calculated as a ratio. Bonds pay a fixed coupon and the yield rises if the price of the bond declines and conversely, the yield falls when the price of the bond rises—as we have experienced in recent years.) Regardless of whether you think bond prices will decline or rise, the fact remains that to grow your assets in a meaningful way over the long-term, stocks must comprise a significant portion of your total portfolio. And, my wise friend in the illustration raised an excellent point. Even if our assets are designated for a future financial goal, chances are what remains will be passed along to our heirs, who by definition have a much longer time horizon.

Intelligent Investing Rule #6: *Since "diversification is the only rational deployment of our ignorance," we must be sure to buy securities that straddle a broad spectrum of economic sectors, to focus on high-quality companies for the long-term and compile a compatible list of 20 or so names that behave well together, especially when things get out of hand.*

ASSET ALLOCATION SUGGESTION FOR AN ETF-ONLY PORTFOLIO

The recommendations offered are based on experience and preference. Any variation that you feel comfortable with is what you should implement.

Education investment account/529 Plan: I would choose a 100 percent allocation to stocks but since the event arrives sooner than most of our long-term financial goals, you may be more comfortable following one of the asset allocation recommendations in chapter 3. Whatever you decide regarding your stock allocation you must also consider which stock segments you want to own and how much in each. Consider the following stock weighting suggestions as a starting point: 40 percent allocation to an S&P 500 ETF; 15 percent to a large-cap dividend ETF; 10 percent to a growth stock ETF; 10 percent each to a mid-cap and small-cap ETF, and 15 percent to an international or global ETF. You can add variations. For example, you may want to increase your international/global exposure and cut your small and mid-cap exposure. Or, you may decide that you don't want that much large-cap exposure and cut your allocation to the S&P 500 fund. As a lover of technology you might determine to add an ETF that indexes the largest holdings in the **NASDAQ**. Or track an industry like banks, or luxury retailers, industrials, or pharmaceuticals. Any segment is available from the various providers of ETFs. (**Note:** if you choose to open a 529 Plan the provider will provide a menu of approved investments to choose from. You may have to vary some from the suggested allocation.)

Retirement investment account: Consider again the asset allocation recommendations offered by our experts in chapter 3 and make your adjustments according to length of time to retirement and (always) what you are comfortable with as an investor. Within that allocation to stocks I would construct a similar portfolio weighting as that of the education account. In my retirement portfolio I have less exposure to the S&P and a greater emphasis on value ETFs. I also have more specialized exposure to a few industry ETFs to complement my individual stock holdings. Other than that, my allocations look a great deal like that recommended for the education account. Again, keep in mind your own risk tolerance and years to retirement as you establish your parameters.

Savings investment account: If you anticipate needing access to this portfolio for more immediate needs like a home, a car, or a grand vacation, ETFs provide excellent liquidity. Your optimal allocation will depend on the estimated timing of those events. Begin with the allocation stated above and modify according to your specific requirements. Rule of thumb: if you think you are going to need the money in the next year or two it is probably best *not* to invest that money in the stock market. If you decide you still want to do so, invest only half. Even if you believe the market will be higher over the ensuing months we can rarely predict with a high enough level of certainty that will in fact be the case and you would hate to find yourself in the position of needing to withdraw money in a declining market. Investing requires a three to five-year time horizon to incubate growth and weather any potential downturns. Additionally, be aware when you are withdrawing money from a savings investment account you will be required to pay taxes on all net gains. And, further, you will pay a much higher rate on short-term gains (less than twelve-month holding period) than you will on a long-term gain (held over twelve months). This tax liability should also be factored into your decision when you are investing taxable savings over short periods of time.

Asset Allocation Suggestions When You Are Employing Stocks and ETFs

I invest about 75 percent of my equity allocation in individual large-cap holdings. And almost 100 percent of those holdings are stocks

I selected employing the value and growth at reasonable price strategies we discussed in previous chapters. Because the research and my experience demonstrate that a concentration of about twenty stocks is optimal, I shoot for that number of holdings. But generally, I target twenty main holdings with an allocation informed by the overall economic sector weightings in the S&P 500. Within those twenty stocks I overweight the very best companies with the very best valuations. Beyond that I allocate 10 percent to a small-cap ETF, 5 percent to a mid-cap ETF, and 10 percent to an international ETF. But, I didn't always have such a large exposure to individual stocks. Like the size of my dining room table my savings grew and as it did I gradually added stocks. I began with twenty-five or fifty shares of a particular stock and then added other stocks and purchased more shares of existing stocks over time. Investing is a process, like decorating my home. I have to live in and with it until eventually I notice a corner that needs a little something or a wall that is too blank. My portfolio is no different. Over time, I learn about new companies I'd like to own, or perceive an area where my portfolio is over- or underexposed and I make the adjustment. But beware: Investing is like being in a perpetual state of discomfort. If I buy shares in a stock and it goes up—I didn't buy enough. If it goes down—I bought too much. That is the immediate response, just as our muscles burn after a rigorous hike or a long run. Still, the discomfort is also the pleasure.

A Word About Tax Strategy

For purposes of this discussion let's stipulate that tax strategy is a-political. I assume that we all pay our fair share and that our primary goal should be the care of own family. It's kind of like the airplane announcement that advises parents to put their own masks on before their children. The first time I heard it I objected to the notion of taking care of myself first then realized I couldn't help my kids if I didn't first ensure the oxygen was flowing to my brain. Maximizing total return for the benefit of your future and the future of your family is my concern and the reason I wrote this book. I will leave it to you and Uncle Sam as to how you settle up.

That said, when we have discussed the returns of stocks in the various studies cited the calculation has been made and stated on a pre-tax basis. When you take gains they are subject to the prevailing tax rules. As of the end of 2013 the taxable rate for long-term capital gains ranges from zero to 20 percent depending on your tax bracket. Short-term capital gains are taxed at your income tax rate. So tax planning is critical to enhancing your long-term capital gains. If you are investing in a 529 college plan or an IRA/401(k) you don't have to worry about taxes. All gains (and losses) are tax exempt. You don't pay taxes on those funds until you begin to withdraw them and they are treated as income in the year(s) you do so. So breathe easy about those funds. You will be able to maximize your total return in a tax-free environment (which, after all makes sense since you have already paid taxes on the acquisition of that money via income tax when you earned it in the first place except in the case of your 401(k) contributions). Your savings account is another story. In this case, though you've paid income taxes on the acquisition of this money as well, you will have to pay again if you generate gains. But you can offset those gains against any losses you've realized. And you can work to ensure all your gains are taxed at the lower, long-term rate.

The rules for **tax loss harvesting**, as it is called, require that you may not buy any security you are selling for tax purposes for over thirty days before or after the sale of the security. This is important because you may have a holding you like for the long-term but have a loss in for the short-term. Selling that stock in order to realize the loss does not preclude you from buying it back. But you must wait thirty days plus one. In this way you can manage the gains you are realizing and their impact on your overall tax liability.

Take heart. There are two reasons for you not to worry extensively about gains and taxes:

1. When you are investing for future goals and buying high-quality companies like those we have been considering you will naturally encounter infrequent need to sell your stocks and realize the gains. In most cases these are stocks to own for a lifetime. Much of our selling will be based on our need to rebalance to our asset allocation policy from time to time.

2. Your discount broker platform will keep track of your unrealized as well as realized gains and losses. Though we have not talked about discount brokers and the information available to you as an investor we will do so briefly now. In addition to providing stock and ETF research, discount brokers facilitate your purchase and sale of investments and keep track of what are called your **tax lots**. Tax lots represent the increments in which you buy and sell securities. Each trade is a tax lot and the broker keeps a schedule of how much you paid for the shares in that particular lot and when you purchased them. Additionally you can view an up-to-date realized gain and loss schedule to assess your tax liability at any time during the year.

I am not suggesting that you should hold onto stocks or ETFs simply to avoid generating taxable gains. Taxes should not dictate your investment strategy. I am simply suggesting that you should be aware when you create a tax liability so you can set aside funds to pay the taxes. Because we are interested in owning stocks for a lifetime or even generations, the turnover in our portfolios will by definition be small.

Composing a balanced, well-behaved portfolio requires planning and an accumulation of knowledge. Nothing can insure us entirely from an unplanned-for calamity but the more prepared we are, the more likely we will meet our goals with minimal disruption or worry. Taking the time to develop a list of high-quality, stable companies and established, low-cost ETFs will put us in the best position possible to meet the daily demands of our lives all the while setting our money to work toward meeting our future financial goals.

CHAPTER 7

Meet Your Research Team: A Smartphone and Sirius XM Radio Account— Accessible and Timely Financial Information for Busy Women

If you spend as much of your life commuting, in carpool lines, or at the airport as I did you have just discovered a block of time in which you can conduct investment research. In addition to the school drop-off and pick-up line, I logged in hours waiting for delayed flights, in check-out lines, and at soccer and baseball games. My son's freshman football coach routinely kept the boys an hour past pick-up and the only thing that prevented me from committing a flagrant personal foul was a stack of *Wall Street Journals* and piles of stock research that kept kept me productively occupied. Today financial information is easily accessible: each of the websites listed in the appendix can be accessed with a smartphone. Financial and news networks are available on satellite radio. As masters of multi-tasking, women today can accomplish a great deal more with the aid of technology than I ever could. I spent plenty of time on those aluminum bleachers; I had no choice but to maximize my time. And so can you, with much less hassle and fuss. And with a smartphone rather than a stack of papers.

So where do you start?

FINANCIAL DATA IS PLENTIFUL AT NO COST TO THE INDIVIDUAL INVESTOR

When I served as a chief investment officer, our annual research budget was millions of dollars. We paid dearly for many sources of data you can now access for free. Of course, the difficulty when there is an abundance of free information available is to determine how to cut through the blizzard of data and opinion and find what you are looking for. Sadly, I have no magic formula. Knowing which site best serves your investing purpose requires time and a little trial and error. But I can share my experiences and you can take what resonates with you and leave what does not.

First and foremost, I don't consult financial websites for opinion. Nor do I act on the investment opinions offered by television pundits. I do, however, pay attention to the factual content published on financial websites and, correspondingly, the factual data presented on financial news networks. A good place to start is with **Stock Rover.**

An Easy to Navigate, Free Portfolio Management Tool

Stock Rover is a free site that allows individual investors to load their stock and ETF portfolio into a format that shows one-day performance in terms of the actual dollars gained or lost and year-to-date returns in percentage. Additionally this portfolio management tool segments your holdings by sector. Dividend yield as well as expected income for each security you hold is listed. Because you input the number of shares you own into the system, you must update the portfolio when you trade (I sometimes have trouble remembering or finding the time to do so but even with a slightly out-of-date portfolio I still find the information very useful). And while this system may be somewhat redundant with the statement your discount broker provides, the analytics Stock Rover provides is much superior. Additionally you can compare your portfolio to those of well-known investors like Warren Buffett, Bill Gates, and Yale University to name a few. You can also conduct stock research and create watch lists. Stock Rover is a robust site that provides unique portfolio management tools as well as broad-based research on individual securities. Version 4—the latest Stock Rover release—allows investors to test their portfolio risk based on sector weightings. A premium service will also be available but the free service will continue to be offered. If you are spreadsheet oriented and like detailed information on your portfolio, Stock Rover is an excellent tool.

WEB-BASED STOCK RESEARCH EASILY ACCESSED BY ANY WEB-ENABLED PHONE OR TABLET

Yahoo! Finance is probably the most user-friendly site for personal investors and provides a comprehensive charting capability that I find very useful. In addition to looking at stocks over the short- and medium-term Yahoo! allows investors to view a stock's performance over a "max" period, which usually dates back to 1960 or 1965. Additionally the charts allow a stock's performance to be compared against another stock's performance or the various stock market indices over the same period. This is very useful in researching prospective stocks. The extended stock performance charting adds perspective to our financial ratios and the stock's current valuation. News and Wall Street recommendations are also available as well as company insider trading data (Figure 7.1).

I mentioned in a previous chapter that I like to use **Bloomberg's** investment site. As a professional investor I used Bloomberg's highly complex and robust institutional site but continue to be impressed with the simplicity of the retail site and the quality of the financial data provided for stocks. Bloomberg.com is where I find data like next year's earnings estimates and the calculations ready-made for the forward p/e (based on next year's earnings), the price-to-sales

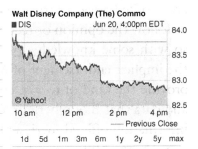

Prev Close:	83.77	Day's Range:	82.79 - 84.08
Open:	84.08	52wk Range:	60.41 - 85.86
Bid:	82.83 × 1300	Volume:	11,073,748
Ask:	83.06 × 500	Avg Vol (3m):	6,386,610
1y Target Est:	88.54	Market Cap:	143.43B
Beta:	1.32	P/E (ttm):	21.31
Next Earnings Date:	5-Aug-14	EPS (ttm):	3.89
		Div & Yield:	0.86 (1.00%)

Figure 7.1 Yahoo! Finance summary page for Walt Disney Company (DIS). Reproduced with permission of Yahoo. ©2014 Yahoo. YAHOO! and the YAHOO! logo are registered trademarks of Yahoo.

ratio, and the p/e to growth or PEG. Here I also find the stock's p/e relative to the p/e of the S&P 500 and the dividend yield as well as dividend payment and growth history. The site also offers company press releases and some of the most comprehensive company news available to investors on the internet.

MarketWatch, *The Wall Street Journal,* and *Barron's* are each published by Dow Jones & Co. MarketWatch is a free site that produces factual news content. And plenty of it. The articles are news driven rather than opinion driven and provide the kind of information investors are interested in seeing on a daily basis. The home page (like *The Wall Street Journal*) contains top national and international as well as financial news written by dedicated journalists; coverage is broad-based, market focused, and viewed by over 16 million visitors each month according to the publisher. But the site is not only limited to news. A section entitled "Industry" focuses on industries and specific companies within those industries, allowing you, the investor, to streamline your research. If you are unable or not inclined to pay to subscribe to *Barron's* or *The Wall Street Journal,* MarketWatch is an essential source of financial and general news that is easily accessed and navigated. And if you don't have the time or interest in navigating a host of sites, MarketWatch also provides a section entitled "Trading Deck" where you can read articles that recommend stocks and reflect the views of the writers. Unlike many of the investing sites that allow contributors to blog with modest oversight from a panel of editors, "Trading Deck" contributors are "market professionals" whose credentials are profiled adjacent to their article. In this way if you determine to follow the opinion or recommendation of the author you can do so with some knowledge of their background and specialty. And the implicit endorsement of MarketWatch. While the site does not provide the kind of robust company financial screening, charting, and data that Bloomberg or Yahoo! Finance provide, the news and information offered merit a place on your favorites list.

Seeking Alpha is a free site staffed with contributors—over 7,000—who are "investors and industry experts rather than **sell-side analysts**." Investors can create a watch list of companies and receive email alerts of breaking news or opinion articles written by one of the sites' contributors. The site actively seeks contributors who can write content that meets the criteria of the site's editors but also prides itself on the the fact that articles "frequently move stocks." Seeking Alpha is popular—especially with traders—and I believe hosts some very good writers and investors. But, if, like me, you don't sit at your desk all day trading your portfolio (and I hope you don't!) the volume of ideas and email alerts is a bit much. Still, if you are interested in trends and identified with the traits I outlined for growth investors, you may want to keep track of what is being written by the trendsetters on Seeking Alpha.

GuruFocus is another free website that offers a unique perspective for the individual investor. This site allows you to see the portfolio of many professional money managers. The subscription version provides investors real-time access to view portfolios of a broader base of professional managers. The site was founded to provide individual investors access to the stocks researched and owned by the best professional investors in the world. Additionally, the site is "dedicated to value investing" based on the belief that value investing is the best strategy for the long-term. Even if you were only able to observe Warren Buffett's portfolio as of the end of the previous quarter, the site would be well worth your time. Of course, Buffett's holdings are widely available (most particularly on Buffett's Berkshire Hathaway site) but GuruFocus provides access to many more managers' portfolios as well as overall industry weightings and recent performance for each stock. If you choose to pay for the premium membership you will have a ready-made platform to screen stocks according to the ratios we examined in previous chapters in addition to real-time access to the professionals' portfolios. But, here again, while the tool is useful we are seeking to own companies for the long haul, to make our decisions deliberately and thoughtfully. The constant temptation for long-term investors is to resist the siren call of the short-term trader or investor and especially the glamorous TV trader pounding his fist on today's great stock idea. Which brings me to television and satellite radio financial news outlets.

THE ALWAYS ON, EVER-READY FINANCIAL NEWS MEDIA

For many years I was a guest on various financial news shows on various networks. I gave interviews to radio show hosts and all kinds of print media. Eventually I was invited to become a regular guest host on CNBC's Squawk Box—a three-hour segment that covered the pre-open and opening of the stock market. And I would be untruthful if I didn't say I enjoyed the experience. The limo pulling up to my hotel at 4:30 in the morning, midtown Manhattan almost peaceful at that time of day. Sitting in the green room prior to the show reviewing the lineup and the guests. The makeup room with the wall-to-wall mirrors framed in those large, bright lightbulbs reminiscent of an old Broadway musical film and the makeup artist who knew my name and just the right color palette to bring my face back to life. Yes, I thoughtfully considered each question posed to me and tried to assert my best ideas when it came to stock recommendations or market prognostications. But how could I really? How can anyone? Without knowing the individual circumstances and goals of those listening how can practitioners and pundits provide insightful and useful recommendations? Only you can make those choices for your portfolio.

So, the trick to watching or listening to financial news is to glean facts. Increasingly the networks are appealing to traders. Folks who desire to make fast money—in fact that is the name of one of the segments on CNBC where traders debate short-term ideas. But we are interested in what the strategists and the companies themselves have to say. Seek out those segments. I watch the early morning show to observe the **stock market futures**, which provide an indication of how the market will open, and to see the development of breaking economics news, which provides perspective on the economy and the business climate facing the companies whose stocks I own. I mute or turn off the segments throughout the rest of the day where short-term ideas are floated and discussed. Then, if possible I return to the last hour of trading and the segment post market close. Here is where I often learn from the company management teams themselves about earnings announcements or new initiatives. Remember that the stocks market opens at 9:30 eastern standard time so for me (on the west coast) I can (and have for decades) watch or listen to the morning market news before or on my way to work. Ditto on the way home.

There are three primary financial news outlets: CNBC, Bloomberg, and Fox Business News. All three are available on most cable platforms and Sirius XM radio. You can listen to as much or as little as you find helpful.

Intelligent Investing Rule #7: *Use financial websites and news for factual content rather than opinions. Only you can decide which investments fit your portfolio and meet your long-term goals.*

I will say this in closing. Despite the fact that I continue to listen to and watch the financial news networks I cannot associate one good long-term idea with doing so. We are all much better off making informed and strategic long-term decisions and letting our investments appreciate over time. There is certainly incremental value in consulting the websites we've reviewed to screen holdings and build our research files on individual stocks or ETFs. But, beware of any source where opinion and stock ideas are hawked.

So what do you say we take an in-depth look at some real-time investment ideas? We'll start with Apple Computer and Coach.

CHAPTER 8

Apple Computer—A Case Study in How to Select a Core Holding: A Role Model Investment You Will Want to Emulate

If you are a woman who makes lists, investing is the perfect opportunity for you to engage in the practice. A number of books have been written on the topic of how to create an investing checklist and though I haven't read a book on the subject, there is certainly merit to the idea of establishing a rigid survey method. Constructing a checklist of quantitative valuation criteria and qualitative product and management criteria lends discipline to decision-making. And discipline is good. In fact, as a professional money manager my team did just that. We measured each company we owned against our checklist of 12 Fundamental Factors. In order for a stock to become eligible for purchase it was required to pass a majority of the factors: three qualitative factors that measured the effectiveness of the management team, the company's "franchise value" (or market and brand dominance), and the relevance of the company's business or products (what I referred to earlier as the buggy-whip factor). The quantitative factors examined valuation ratios like those we have discussed, among other things. The inspiration for our development of the 12 Factor model was to limit our exposure to stocks that are "cheap for a good reason": the ultimate value trap.

As investors we must be on guard against value traps. Just as we have all fallen prey to the illusion in our private lives, whether we bite or not depends on our awareness of the hazard and our discipline in avoiding it. In my case, I've sworn off clearance sales because I am prone to buying things I don't need. Or items that are damaged, or inferior. In the frenzy of cheap prices my judgment risks becoming impaired. I studiously avoid infomercials because I am a sucker for skincare product propaganda. Tell me a moisturizer is proven to increase the elasticity of my skin and I'm in, whole hog. Inevitably, I find the product is powerless against the laws of gravity and I face the hassle of unwinding the automatic re-order required at the time of purchase. Establishing investment rules, a checklist, criteria—whatever you want to call it—aids in minimizing risk and increases your chances of avoiding value traps.

For our purposes, we don't need twelve factors but we could use a handful that will keep us focused and on track. Valuation, of course, should be first and foremost on our list but, as we have discussed, the danger in considering only valuation is the risk that we may end up with a stock that is cheap for good reason. Over the years I have found the most compelling factors in determining "cheap for good reason" are those that measure the relevance and sustainability of the company's product offering, the quality of the management team, and the corporate culture and franchise value. Great companies are market and brand dominators who should eventually solve their problems even if they lag in innovation for a time, (though there are occasional exceptions). All of these are qualitative factors we can measure on our own, which is the good news and the bad news. Much of what goes into my decision-making is inferred from observation, reading, and familiarity with the company. You will find with some stocks one of the factors may not be relevant—product innovation matters less if a company produces a commodity like oil or gasoline—so you will put more emphasis on other issues like the quality of the management team. The qualitative factors cannot be plugged into a ratio like price and earnings or sales. But women have good instincts and we understand how to weigh and juggle a variety of variables. Establishing and evaluating qualitative factors will come naturally to most of us, perhaps more naturally than evaluating financial ratios.

IMPLEMENTING OUR INVESTMENT STRATEGY IN REAL TIME; A BRIEF PRIMER ON APPLE COMPUTER

So let's move from the hypothetical to the actual. Whether we are building our portfolio for a more immediate goal like our young child's college education or a future retirement, identifying core holdings in paramount. A core holding is a stock we can be comfortable owning over a reasonably short period of time (three to five years) or an even longer-term period (ten to twenty years). Core holdings are stocks that while they may have underperformed in the short-term have the financial and management tools to right the ship. Let's examine a classic Fallen Angel growth stock and potential core holding: Apple Computer (**stock ticker**: AAPL).

Because of Apple's attractive valuation, brand dominance (franchise value), technological innovation (buggy-whip factor), and experienced management team the stock has the potential to become a core holding. The kind of stock you can build your portfolio around. But before we take a look at valuation let's review the reasons the stock became cheap in the first place and in doing so we will have a better understanding of where the company stands in relation to our checklist of factors important to us.

A little history: This former growth stock darling fell out of favor with investors over the last year or so (ending 2013). But if we were to review a chart of the historical price appreciation of AAPL we would see that the performance of this stock since its public offering in 1980 has been nothing short of remarkable. Certainly there have been times (like the recent period) where Apple's stock price has underperformed for a period but over the long-term these troughs have provided investors with an attractive opportunity to invest in the stock. Since December 31, 1982 when the earliest data is available, the stock has produced an annual return of 18.0 percent versus 11.4 percent for the S&P 500. But, as is often the case, during a period of underperformance like the recent one, the management team has come under fire. Similar to many managers of great companies the new CEO, Tim Cook, who took over for Steve Jobs, has faced some difficulties. And, perhaps, because he followed the iconic Jobs, Cook has also faced a host of critics. The company's ability to innovate has similarly been doubted by analysts—what comes after the iPhone and iPad they wonder? And, finally, worries over Apple's ability to dominate the smartphone market have emerged as Samsung gains share, particularly in the low price point category.

Apple's stock peaked just above $700.00 in September of 2012. At that time Wall Street analysts loved the company and most had a buy rating on the stock. The company's stock appreciated to the point where it became the most valuable American company of all time, surpassing Exxon Mobil as the largest company measured by **market capitalization** (which is simply the stock price multiplied by the number of shares outstanding). The run-up in the stock was largely due to the anticipation surrounding the iPhone 5 announcement. Consumers loved the new phone and the company received two million pre-orders in the first 24 hours. Investors were enthusiastic because orders for the iPhone 5 doubled the first-day orders over the previous year's launch of the 4S. One analyst interviewed by *Money* magazine said that while his price target for the stock was $690 (and the stock closed that day at $701.91) the historically high price for the stock was justified and that future earnings would support the price momentum in the stock. In other words, despite the fact his own valuation work showed that the stock was overvalued, like most investors who allow themselves to be influenced by recency effect and momentum—he loved it even more at the higher price. The next day the stock began an almost eight-month slide, bouncing off a low of around $390 and traded range-bound for months.

THE QUESTION TO ASK: IS APPLE CHEAP FOR GOOD REASON?

A premium product known for its quality and leading-edge technology, Apple's uncharacteristic blunder—removing Google Maps from the new iOS software release—opened the floodgates of doubt and criticism about the company post Steve Jobs and about the leadership of Tim Cook. Two months later a headline read: "Apple's Stock Price Crashes To Six Month Low And There's No Bottom in Sight." Investors had fallen out of love and were selling the stock. Often stocks will run-up in anticipation of a new product launch like the iPhone 5 and then sell off once the announcement is made, the old "buy on the rumor sell on the news" adage. But Apple investors didn't just sell, they bailed. And the maps debacle catalyzed the frenzy. Once the drumbeats start, the volume inevitably rises. And suddenly Wall Street analysts and portfolio managers who loved the stock months or for that matter just weeks ago, now found fundamental problems with the company's ability to continue to develop innovative products. Apple, suddenly, was almost universally hated. The rapidity of the change in sentiment was breathtaking.

On January 24, 2013, AAPL plunged another 12 percent to $450 after posting the slowest profit growth since 2003. The company reported that sales rose 18 percent but profit rose only 1 percent because of higher costs. In the following weeks as the overall market rallied, the stock declined further. The first stumble with Google Maps (as is often the case) was not the last. Then in March of 2013 in an effort to stave off some of the criticism and increase shareholder value, the company announced a dividend increase of 15 percent, resulting in a dividend yield well above the yield of the S&P 500. Yet, the selling continued. Some thought the dividend increase did not go far enough because of the enormous stockpile of cash on Apple's balance sheet (from the end of 2012 until the spring of 2013 when the dividend increase was announced, Apple's cash hoard grew from approximately $120 billion to $145 billion, more than the gross domestic product of many countries). The company also announced an increase to their $10 billion **share repurchase program**, adding another $50 billion to the program but nothing seemed to satisfy investors and the stock deteriorated further. (Investors are usually cheered by share repurchase programs because fewer shares means greater earnings per share reported and attributed to the remaining shares.) It was about this time I began to take a look at adding to my Apple stock. As we have learned, the best time to consider buying a Fallen Angel growth stock is after it has passed from love to disappointment to hate, finally, wallowing in neglect.

By the summer of 2013 the stock seemed to be more than reflecting Wall Street's concerns and on July 22, with the stock languishing near recent lows of just above $400 per share, the right question seemed to be the one raised by the fabled Peter Lynch—would we allow the market to scare us out of a great company? I posted the following on my blog: "With AAPL yielding 2.8% (more than the ten year treasury which is hovering below 2.5%) and earnings estimated at $39.44 per share in 2013 growing to a consensus estimate of $43.37 in 2014, the stock trades at a price-to-earnings ratio of 9.9 times 2014 earnings. Whether Apple is the right stock for you depends on many things including what you already own and your investing time horizon. I only use it as an example of a cheap stock hated by the Wall Street crowd. Had you followed the advice being offered by the experts last fall you would have lost approximately $274 per share or about 40% on your investment. Now might be a good time to at least take a look, while the crowd is looking the other way."

Not a lot had to go right for Apple to become of interest to investors in July of 2013. This is often the case with great companies when their stock is acting badly. Good things happen.

A brief digression: This is a good place to consider the company's buggy-whip or product relevance factor. Chances are you likely have at least one Apple product or an Apple-inspired product in your home. You may not own an iPod but AAPL's innovation in the MP3 player space improved the user experience for all digital music listeners. The same can be argued if you use a touch-screen smartphone or a tablet—also Apple innovations. It is true that many former innovators like Eastmann Kodak, Xerox, or Polaroid, to name a few, have become largely irrelevant—the risk always exists that a company will rest so comfortably on their past technological laurels that they will experience a fatal stumble. The question for you to consider is whether you believe that is true for Apple. It is always possible, but is it likely?

Eventually, Carl Icahn announced a position in Apple—a big one. (His portfolio is one you can view on GuruFocus.) And the stock shot up over $20 per share. Once he announced his position (in a Tweet no less) Wall Street investors began jumping in though the company hadn't materially changed. Rather, a badly performing stock of a great company finally caught the eye of Wall Street. We want to *already* be in position when Wall Street becomes interested. We want to be nibbling away at the bad stocks of great companies before the crowd charges in. Icahn's involvement was also a boost for Tim Cook. Icahn made it clear he wanted to work with management (not oust them) to discuss strategies for increasing shareholder value. He went out of his way to support Cook's management of the company.

Gradually investor mood began to shift and the stock continued to climb out of its hole. By September 11 of 2013 when Apple unveiled the iPhone 5C (their new lower price point offering) and the iPhone5S the stock had appreciated over 20 percent from late summer. After the new product announcement the stock dropped 6 percent on the news, as often happens. But once the sales numbers for the new phones were revealed and investors understood that earnings growth would continue, the stock resumed its methodical move up above $500. I cannot, nor am I intending to, predict where the stock might be at the time of publication of this book. Rather, my illustration intends to emphasize the way Wall Street responds to companies that disappoint. It becomes personal. Which brings us back to where we started.

In 2012 and 2013, Apple was dead money, the funeral dirge for former darlings. Getting to know a company during that lonely period of neglect is a luxury available to those of us interested in buying growth stocks at reasonable values. Once the fury of bad news is past no one wants to talk about the stock any longer—unless, of course, it is to complain. Despite the move up in the stock during the second half of 2013 Apple is still attractive.

Since we are considering the stock as one of our potential core holdings let's turn our close attention to the valuation.

VALUATION REVEALS A GREAT DEAL ABOUT INVESTOR EXPECTATIONS, AN OPPORTUNITY FOR SAVVY INVESTORS

My first stop is Yahoo! Finance. There I find a heading entitled key statistics. I note that the forward p/e for AAPL is around 11.5x versus the p/e of 9.9x forward earnings the stock sported in the summer of 2013. This increase in the p/e is due to the stock's appreciation off the lows of summer. (We call this **multiple expansion,** which means the stock price is rising faster than the earnings are growing. This often happens to Fallen Angel growth stocks when they begin to recover. So, within reason it is a good thing. And Apple's multiple expansion has certainly risen at a reasonable pace.) But Apple still trades well below the p/e for the S&P 500, which is trading at around 16x 2014 earnings estimates. You may hear some analysts or pundits quote an even lower p/e for Apple. This is because they are backing out Apple's enormous cash hoard. The logic goes that if I buy the entire company for say $3 trillion but receive in the transaction Apple's balance sheet, which holds net cash of around $145 billion, then I am really paying $3 trillion less $145 billion or $2.9 trillion for the company. Lowering the stock price to reflect the cash in turn lowers the p/e and makes the stock even cheaper in the eyes of some investors. Either way: Apple's p/e multiple argues that the stock boasts an attractive valuation. Even after appreciating off the 2013 summer lows.

GET TO KNOW THE COMPETITION

When considering valuation we should always be comparing our measurement against something. To understand Apple's valuation—what it is telling us—we must get to know not only the company but also its competition, and continue to dig through the research comparing Apple's growth rate and financial ratios to other stocks in the category. Yahoo! Finance makes this easy. Click on "competitors" in the left margin when viewing Apple stock and you will find the company's competitors defined as Hewlett Packard, BlackBerry, and Google. For simplicity's sake we will assume that Google is Apple's most formidable and relevant competitor. This assumption would be consistent with the comparison made by most analysts; when slugging it out for investor "mindshare" Apple is frequently set against Google (**stock ticker: GOOGL**).

On a p/e basis, GOOGL trades at a premium to the market (and double the multiple investors have applied to Apple) at 24x next year's earnings. When we look at the p/s ratio we find that Google once again trades at a premium to AAPL. Apple's p/s ratio comes in at just under 3x, which means that investors are willing to pay 3x the sales generated by Apple. In Google's case, investors are willing to pay much more. GOOGL trades at a p/s ratio of over 6x revenues. Why would investors be willing to pay double for Google's sales than they are for AAPL's and also double for the earnings produced by GOOGL? The only logical reason is that investors are expecting Google to grow twice as fast as Apple. When investors set high expectations the onus is on Google to produce stellar results. Apple, on the other hand, has only to produce results better than the very low expectations set by Wall Street.

The comparison continues to show more optimistic expectations for GOOGL based on the PEG (price/earnings to growth ratio). Remember, the PEG tells us how much investors are willing to pay not just for earnings (that is what the p/e tells us) but earnings growth. And again investors are willing to pay a premium for Google with a five-year expected PEG of 1.5x versus 0.9x for Apple. When comparing the financial ratios (I found all of this information on Yahoo! Finance) we see across the board, investor expectations that Google will grow about double the rate of Apple. But the market isn't static. And we know that good things often happen to the bad stocks of great companies.

LOWERED EXPECTATIONS AND PRODIGAL COMPANIES

Consider Fallen Angel growth stocks like Apple as if they were prodigals, with the potential to disappoint, certainly, but also to exceed expectations. If and when they do repent, their movement in the right direction may be met with unbridled enthusiasm from Wall Street. We've all experienced it—the always late colleague who finally shows up on time, a self-absorbed friend who suddenly looks you in the eye and asks how *you* are doing, the complaining teenager who out of the blue offers to help around the house. People (and companies) who have lowered our expectations through their behavior have an immense capacity to pleasantly surprise us.

The question you will be asking yourself and attempting to answer through your research is the following: Will Google continue to be twice as attractive as Apple as a long-term grower? To answer that question affirmatively you must believe that Apple's products are on the wane and Google's are sustainably accelerating. You have to believe that Apple's innovation may, in fact, be over. That the next new new thing is more likely to come from Google than Apple. That is what the numbers are telling you. And in order for that to be true over the long-term you must suspend belief in Apple's power as an innovator and marketing and brand leader. You must assume that the approximately $145 billion on the company's balance sheet will fail to add to shareholder value through increased dividends, share repurchase programs, research and development, or strategic acquisitions. You must believe, in essence, that Apple is through leading the industry and growing at above-market levels.

But here is the good news. Even if that is true, Apple is being offered to you at valuation levels that are not only half of Google's valuation but also below what investors are willing to pay for the S&P 500 index. Apple's valuation is telling you that the broad-based index of companies in the S&P is more likely to grow and perform better than Apple. If AAPL is indeed cheap for a good reason—and this is the most important part—and remains cheap for a good reason in the future then the current valuation is correct. But if Apple is actually in the process of reaccelerating the product cycle and earnings growth then this valuation is an opportunity to buy a great company at a discount.

PAYING ATTENTION TO NEWS SOURCES CAN INFORM YOUR DECISION OF WHETHER TO BUY OR NOT BUY

Remember to focus on fact, rather than opinion. The determination we need to make—and, again, this is where your judgment and knowledge of history come into play—is whether Apple is cheap for a good reason or in the process of returning to its mean performance? Over the preceding five years (including the dismal 2012 period) earnings have grown approximately 34 percent per year. But that is not enough for us to know; we need to understand the trajectory of the trend line. One of the things that troubled investors in 2012 was that 2013 earnings reports were projected to be below the extraordinary levels achieved in 2012. The market looks forward not backward, because the market anticipates, or at least attempts to anticipate events. So, the forward trend in earnings is important to Wall Street and a temporary decline in the trajectory may create a potential entry point. I am not, however, suggesting you get into the earnings estimating business. The question for us is broader: can the company fix the problem and restore future earnings growth? Wall Street's time horizon is usually tomorrow, ours is much much longer. And that provides us with an advantage.

From reading the websites listed earlier and scanning news stories in *The Wall Street Journal* and *Barron's* I discovered the following: Since the September release of the iPhone 5C, Apple unveiled the iPad Air in October to subsequent rave reviews. The new iPad Mini with Retina display was released in November. And while many were worried about growth for Apple in the Asian market because of tough competition from Samsung and the lack (until the 5C) of a lower price point smartphone, Apple was quietly building a significant presence in the Japanese market, which has emerged as the company's fastest-growing region and produces the heftiest profit margins. In the last year sales to the Japanese market grew 27 percent and margins exceeded 50 percent compared to 35 percent for the rest of the world. During the period of investor neglect management was doing exactly what they get paid to do—manage the company. Just as Coca Cola investors punished the stock for consumption slowdown in the United States and didn't consider the potential for Coke in Europe in the late 1970s, investors may be extrapolating Apple's recent stumbles and estimating stalled earnings growth out into infinity. Doing so ignores what we learned in the first chapter: reversion to the mean. I am willing to bet, I should say invest, that Apple will eventually return to its mean performance of growth as well as once more become an industry leader in technological innovation. And until they do, this inexpensive potential core holding trades at half the valuation of its primary competitor (GOOGL) and well below that of the S&P 500. Importantly, while waiting for the stock to recover, Apple pays a hefty dividend each and every quarter. (Since writing AAPL stock price has increased significantly—almost 30 percent—and GOOGL has declined slightly.)

If you decide to begin accumulating Apple as a core holding, the dividend, in addition to providing total return, will provide a shortcut to the earnings question by telling you what management and the board of directors think about the future. During the company's bleakest months of 2013, the board raised the dividend 15 percent to $3.05 per share (or $12.20 per share per year) where it sits today. It is reasonable to expect another increase in 2014 and reasonable to deduce management will be signaling future earnings growth with that increase. And, of course, you will be pocketing a nice return while you wait for the market to agree with you about AAPL's future. (Apple declared a 7-for-1 stock split effective in early June and another high single-digit dividend increase.)

Apple is the kind of stock we want to at least consider as a core holding in our portfolio. An industry and brand dominator that the market seems to be ignoring. Starbucks in 2009, Tiffany in 2012, and Disney, Nike, and Nordstrom in recent years (all stocks I own). Former growth darlings who have been underestimated by investors and have provided value-oriented investors with a once-in-a-decade opportunity to own the shares of great companies at compelling prices. These are the kinds of stocks we can build a portfolio around and that we can plan to own for a lifetime.

Intelligent Investing Rule #8: *Focusing on specific qualitative and valuation factors will allow you to avoid Terminally Cheap stocks. Step back from the Wall Street hype as you determine if a Fallen Angel growth stock is an incredible buy or cheap for a good reason. Use periods of underperformance to find great, long-term investment opportunities and don't let the "market scare you out of them."*

ETF CORE HOLDING OPTIONS FOR THOSE WHO ARE PRESSED FOR TIME

But what if you say, as I have said on so many occasions: "I don't have time for this. I don't have time to conduct research on a core holding like Apple." Well don't you worry. We have a solution for that as well—a low-cost, diversified solution that still provides you with exposure to potential core holdings like Apple. ETF offerings from PowerShares, iShares, Schwab, and Vanguard provide varying exposure to Apple and stocks in traditional growth sectors like information technology, consumer discretionary, and health care. Let's first take a look at the PowerShares QQQ (**ticker:** QQQ).

This ETF seeks to track the Nasdaq-100 Index and usually consists of all 100 stocks in the index that represent large US and non-US "nonfinancial companies" listed on the Nasdaq exchange. As of the middle of December 2013 the top holdings in the fund were Apple Inc. (12.60 percent), Microsoft Corp. (7.69 percent), Google Inc. (7.58 percent), Amazon.com Inc. (4.60 percent), and Intel Corp. (3.19 percent). As you can see, simply by owning the QQQ you will receive strong exposure to Apple while at the same time receiving diversification across other large and well-known companies. The next five largest holdings are QUALCOMM Inc., Cisco Systems Inc., Gilead Sciences Inc., Comcast Corp., and Facebook Inc. Visit the PowerShares website and you can review a fact sheet that provides the fund's largest holdings (and the entire portfolio) as well as the overall sector weightings. The total expense ratio is listed at 0.20 percent. Because of the tech-heavy index the fund tracks, exposure to information technology is at 55 percent of the total portfolio, which is nearly twice that of the other funds we will consider. This is important for you to know and to keep in mind as you determine which ETF suits your objectives. Technology stocks can generate spectacular performance and spectacular volatility.

The iShares S&P 500 Growth ETF (**ticker:** IVW) tracks the large-cap growth sector of the US equity market. The top five holdings in the fund (when I went to the iShares website) were: Apple Inc. (5.60 percent), Google Inc. (3.17 percent), Exxon Mobil Corp. (2.64 percent), Bank of America Corp. (1.92 percent), and Coca-Cola Co. (1.87 percent). As you can see, these top five holdings provide much broader sector exposure, with information technology accounting for only 26.8 percent of the total fund. The fund fee is 0.18 percent. The remaining two ETFs are offered by Schwab and Vanguard respectively. The Schwab US Large-Cap Growth ETF (**ticker:** SCHG) seeks to track the Dow Jones US Large-Cap Growth Total Stock Market Index. This index is comprised of stocks with "growth style characteristics." The fund's expense ratio is 0.07 percent (significantly lower than the QQQ and IVW funds) and allocates around 27 percent to information technology, with Apple, by far, the largest holding at 5.7 percent of fund assets. As is the case with the IVW fund, the SCHG sector allocations are more broadly distributed; the top ten holdings are also diversified among names like Amazon, Berkshire Hathaway (Warren Buffett's company), Comcast, Johnson & Johnson, Pepsico, and Wal-Mart. Lastly, the Vanguard Growth ETF (VUG) shares a similar objective as the SCHG, with a slightly higher fee at 0.10 percent. Again, the largest holding is Apple at 6.22 percent and the fund offers similar sector allocations to those of the SCHG.

Go to Yahoo! Finance yourself and graph the performance of the four funds. You can compare them over a variety of time periods all on the same chart. The basic charting capability offered by Yahoo! allows you to enter as many fund or stock tickers as you like as well as a relevant index. In this way you can compare the performance and volatility of whatever ETF or stock you desire to examine and make an informed decision regarding which investment might suit your investment objective: a core holding like Apple or an ETF (or both). I decided to graph the performance of Apple over the most recent two-year period, which—as we know—has been a difficult one for the company while comparing its performance to the performance of our four ETFs.

Apple exhibited the heart-thumping volatility we've already discussed compared to the more muted volatility of the four ETFs. Over the last two years the steadier, less "exciting" performance of one of the funds might be preferable. But compared over the last five years AAPL significantly outperforms each fund, though they all perform admirably. Which investment you choose will depend entirely on the amount of time you are willing to put into the research of your core holdings and your tolerance for the roller-coaster-like movement we can see in Fallen Angel growth stocks like Apple in the short-term.

Either way, as you build your portfolio and keep your long-term goals in mind you will necessarily make choices resulting in various trade-offs. For portfolios with a shorter life span (like college education funds) you may not be interested in being exposed to the potentially higher volatility of a core holding like Apple as I am, or any individual stock for that matter. ETFs may serve the objective much more effectively. In a long-term retirement portfolio, higher risk might appeal to you. You have the time to tolerate volatility and the appetite to increase your total return. A core holding like Apple might match your long-term objective. With accessible and free tools (like Yahoo! Finance and others) available to research qualitative and valuation factors, to chart historical performance, and compare investment opportunities we most certainly have the ability (if not always the time) to make informed decisions regarding individual stocks and ETFs that can form the core of our portfolios.

A reminder: As you consider which securities will form the core of your portfolio avoid the trap of making the decision to buy a stock by the actual dollar price alone. By now, I believe you are sophisticated enough to select stocks based on our valuation criteria, but as a reminder don't avoid stocks like Apple simply because the stock price is in the hundreds of dollars. Absolute price alone should never encourage or deter you. Our valuation factors have taught us that the determination of value is based on the stock price compared to the company's earnings—what we are paying for a company's future earnings—not merely how much a share of the stock costs in absolute dollars. Believing a stock is cheap because it trades for $15 is a fallacy. Just as fallacious is the conclusion that another stock is expensive because it trades for ten times that amount. There is no investing rule that says you must purchase 100 shares of a stock to hold it in your portfolio. You can buy one share if that is all you have the funds for. And you will participate proportionately in the stock's price movement. Countless times individual investors have told me that a stock is cheap or expensive based solely on the absolute dollar price of the security rather than its valuation and that lack of understanding is dangerous to their wealth.

CHAPTER 9

A Case Study of a Stalled Luxury Brand— Coach, Inc.: Whether Coach Bags Fit Your Budget or Style, We Can Learn a Great Deal from This Former Darling

Investing is analogous to many things. Most investors are loathe to make the comparisons, though. They want investing to sound smart. Clever. Difficult. They need for their clients to think they are incredibly well-informed and working so very hard to protect and grow their assets. The mystique also serves to create a kind of intellectual barrier to entry. The higher the better as far as the entrenched professionals are concerned. I know, I once played the game. We used phrases like "secular trend" vs. "cyclical trend" or "portfolio alpha" as opposed to the "portfolio beta." We tossed in a standard deviation or two, a reference to the negative or perfect correlation of two investments, and if we really wanted to ratchet up the intellectual superiority (or render our clients entirely somnam-bulant) we talked about the bond market and the yield curve. The pièce de résistance? Convexity. We usually lost them there and felt a kernel of the smug satisfaction physicists must feel when explaining the Theory of Relativity.

So at the risk of betraying the sacred brotherhood allow me to offer some simple yet relevant comparisons as we consider another case study of a potential holding to add to our portfolio: Investing is like raising children. You do the hard work – and plenty of it – for many years without reaping tangible results. A good portion of what you do is based on your instincts and your knowledge of good and bad behaviors, the character and bents of the child, and an awareness of the society they will function in. Though you may have confidence in your approach you may not see results for years. Faith and the passage of time are necessary components.

Investing is also a good bit like dieting (though I cringe at the cliche). There's no secret really, you simply consume less than you burn up each day and you will lose weight—akin to the investing mantra: buy low, sell high. But here again the pros have created a myriad of ways to make the process much more complex and supposedly scientific and, in some cases, even medically supervised. But the equation never alters. Calories consumed minus calories expended equals weight gained or lost. Period.

Investing is also analogous to buying a house. The neighborhood matters, as does the price and condition of the home. Quality factors into the price you are willing to pay, the obvious defects as well. You make an informed decision, move in, and harbor the confidence that eventually your home, which is also a real estate investment, will appreciate. You don't stop thinking about ways to improve your home all the while but you stop worrying about whether you should have made the investment at all—because you have carefully researched it and now the point is to make sure you do all you can to continue to enhance your long-term return. All of these are useful analogies and comparisons to keep in mind when we feel overwhelmed by the knowledge we need or don't have or think we should have. Investing, like life, is an iterative process. So what do we do when we encounter a stock like Coach Inc.?

A LITTLE HISTORY

Coach, Inc. is a stock investors have been scared away from. One misstep after another has pummeled the stock price in recent years. After the company went public in 2000, investors embraced Coach with open arms and continued their love affair until early 2012. Sure, the stock corrected with the market during the financial crisis in 2008 and 2009 but then it resumed its inexorable march upward until early 2012. From October 6, 2000 through the end of 2013 Coach (**stock ticker:** COH) returned 2,340.48 percent compared to a total return of 62.67 percent for the S&P 500. This dramatic outperformance covers two extended periods of underperformance including the most recent lackluster period beginning in 2012 (and still in place as of the writing of this book). A Fallen Angel growth stock, COH has passed through the four stages of investor sentiment: love, disappointment, hate, and neglect.

After years of beating earnings projections, Coach in some ways became a victim of their own success—the handbag business is a growing and lucrative market. In 2011 Americans spent $8.5 billion on handbags and according to Coach their handbag sales had been growing about 10 percent per year compared to overall women's apparel growth of approximately 4 percent per year. But it was Coach's greater than 70 percent profit margins that attracted competition. In August of 2012, after growing sales an average of 14 percent during the previous four years and beating Wall Street revenue estimates in 85 percent of the quarters reported over the previous five years, Coach missed its own estimates and that of analysts. By a wide margin. The stock subsequently experienced its biggest drop in greater than ten years and declined close to 20 percent in an overall rising market. The reason was competition from Michael Kors (**stock ticker:** KORS) for one. KORS had recently gone public and reported a sales increase of 37 percent in the most recent quarter compared to growth of 1.7 percent for COH. Analysts expect that the trend will continue into 2014. Over the last two years Michael Kors' stock trajectory looks like the mirror image of Coach, rising as fast as (or faster than) Coach's stock has declined.

Coach's disappointing sales and earnings results continued for another year before the board announced significant changes to the senior management team. Consequently the stock continued to perform abysmally during a period when the market was hitting historical highs. When the management changes, which included not only a leadership change but also a change in the fashion direction of the brand, finally emerged investors responded with modest enthusiasm. Which is where we are at the time of this writing. A change in leadership is a bold and somewhat desperate effort by the board to inject new life into a flagging company and in this case a flagging brand. When the industry trailblazer and leader finds itself in the situation Coach faces of 1–2 percent top line growth compared to the insurgent, Michael Kors reporting sales growth of 37 percent, all options are on the table.

DOES COACH MEET OUR QUALITATIVE FACTORS?

While waiting for the brand to reignite with consumers, the company continues to manage the underlying business. They will grow outlet square footage in the United States, which generates 60 percent of North American sales and continue to expand in Asia where the premium handbag and accessories market exceeds $12 billion dollars and is expected to generate 50 percent of growth in the coming years. Importantly, global growth also produces higher margins than in the United States. In the meantime the stock has risen about 20 percent from the lows but remains well off the highs. Investors are no longer fleeing the stock but they certainly aren't loading up either. Still, the board and management team made the potentially right and very difficult decision to reallocate human resources to better advantage for the company's future, but the new team is unproven. The brand, though a little saggy, is still the industry leader. Because the product has become stale and promotional, a great deal rests on the shoulders of the new lead designer—also unproven. Still, despite the fact that the product has suffered from design and fashion misses, it still retains the cachet of a global premium brand. Changes are in process but the results not yet measurable. At this stage it is difficult to conclude that COH meets or passes our qualitative factors. For us to make a sound determination about whether the stock is right for our portfolio, we must examine the valuation.

COACH AND THE VALUATION METRICS

When assessing a stock's valuation we often consider the comparative metrics to its primary competitors. In Coach's case, competition is difficult to measure since the company's primary competitor, Michaels Kors, is a very recent entrant into the public market and, consequently, its metrics provide limited perspective. The other dominant competitors—Kate Spade and Dooney & Burke—are private companies whose metrics are unavailable. So we will cobble together our own modest little universe of comparable companies. For example, Tiffany (**stock ticker:** TIF) is a useful comparison to Coach as the ultimate purveyor of luxury items and Nordstrom (**stock ticker:** JWN), a high-end retailer, serves as a relevant benchmark of consumer spending for nonessential or luxury goods. These two companies, while not perfect comps, will lend some perspective from a valuation standpoint on retailers serving a similar market.

As we will see, Coach, unlike Apple, presents a conflicting valuation picture. Because the company's prior sales and earnings are depressed (which is one of the primary reasons the stock is down) the ratios can become somewhat skewed. However, if we begin by looking at the forward p/e we gain a fairly accurate picture of what we are paying for the stock. At the end of 2013 COH trades at a p/e of just under 15x 2014 earnings. TIF trades at 24x and JWN at 16.7x. Coach is trading just shy of the S&P 500's and Nordstrom's p/e ratio; the p/e is overstated by the company's stalled earnings and the market is saying at this point, we are willing to place the floor on the stock here (at 15x earnings) while management sorts through the mess. Because we know the company is in a recovery mode, and yet we have no guarantee when the earnings will actually recover, we cannot place too much emphasis on its p/e, but we also can't ignore it. The bounce back in the company's earnings is not likely to take place in 2014, though the second half should prove better than the first half. Investors may have to wait until 2015. At around 15x 2014's depressed earnings it is difficult to say that the stock price reflects true value. Apple was experiencing a deceleration in earnings in 2013 but the stock price and the p/e (at 9x) reflected that slowdown (which was much shorter lived and much less dramatic than COH's has been). Coach is trading at a multiple about in line with the overall market, which is growing much faster. When we focus on our group of competitors we see that TIF's p/e of 24 reflects the kind of premium investors are willing to pay for a growing luxury brand (year over year quarterly earnings growth is up almost 50 percent) and by that measure, COH (if we believe it will grow again) is trading at a severe discount. But JWN at 16x trades slightly below the median p/e for the industry because of overall concerns about consumer spending rather than a

company-specific problem like Coach's. When all aspects are considered, I would say the stock comes closer to failing than passing
this valuation factor. We must look elsewhere for clues.

The p/s ratio is much more difficult for Coach because it is trading at a high p/s of 3.1x times trailing twelve month sales. Yes, sales
growth has been difficult and so this backward-looking measure
mostly just tells us what we already know (according to Yahoo!
Finance year over year quarterly sales growth has declined 0.90 percent). But it may also be indicating that the valuation is not cheap
based on the underlying fundamentals of the company. Without
a reliable way to estimate future sales growth ourselves we have
to rely somewhat on this backward looking indicator. Compared
to our universe of competitors, both of whom have been growing
sales—JWN is trading at a p/s ratio of 0.96x and TIF at 2.9x—
Coach is trading at a p/s premium and so fails this valuation factor.
Similarly, Coach does not appear cheap based on a price/earnings
to growth basis – the PEG ratio. Trading at a PEG of 1.5x compared to Nordstrom also at 1.5x and Tiffany at 1.7x, Coach's ratio
again fails to provide any compelling insight regarding whether or
not the valuation is attractive. In fact, based on this metric, the
stock looks fairly valued and therefore fails the PEG valuation factor. COH remains the market share leader in its segment but is
losing ground to KORS. The new management have impressive
backgrounds but are, as yet, unproven leading COH. The valuation
factors—though measuring a stock whose sales and earnings have
disappointed and whose price has stalled—still indicate the stock
is, at least, fairly valued, if not expensive compared to its peers. The
market seems to be taking a "wait and see" attitude as to whether
the company can reignite enthusiasm for the product and growth
in sales. Uncertainty prevails. So we improvise. Another strength
of the women I know.

We know that Coach stock peaked at just under $80 per share
by looking at a historical chart on Yahoo! Finance (see figure 9.1).
We also know it declined to around $47 per share in the spring of
2013 or a roughly 40 percent slide. Since then the stock has been
bouncing around in a trading range of plus or minus 20 percent.
Much, or at least some, of the bad news seems to be reflected in

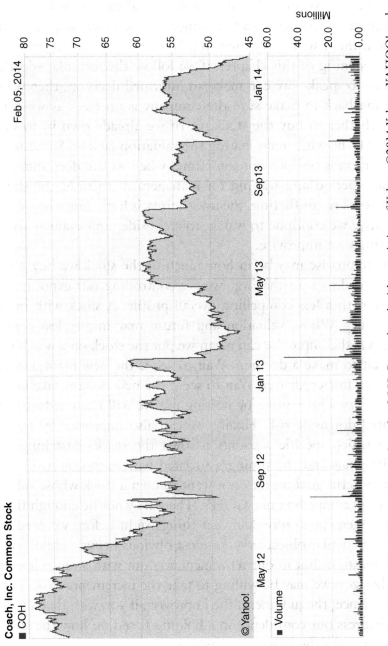

Figure 9.1 Yahoo! Finance price chart for COH. Reproduced with permission of Yahoo. ©2014 Yahoo. YAHOO! and the YAHOO! logo are registered trademarks of Yahoo.

the stock. But there are few believers as is often the case when a Fallen Angel has fallen. The question we must now ask ourselves is: do we believe that Coach, like many Fallen Angels before it, will retain its premier brand ranking and restore earnings growth momentum or will it succumb to failure? Like the analogies cited in the opening of this chapter, if we follow the formula—do the work so to speak—we can make an informed decision, then wait, checking back to make sure the company is on track as we consider whether to buy the stock, or (if we already own it) to buy more. All the while reevaluating the valuation factors. Sometimes the decision is obvious but sometimes when we are deep into the "neglect period and waiting for management to right the ship" the factors are conflicting, the uncertainty is high. Since investing is iterative we continue to watch, to reconsider and evaluate. And sometimes we improvise.

The improvise may be in how much of the stock we buy if we choose to do so. In that way we are controlling our exposure to a stock with a less compelling overall profile. A stock with more uncertainty. Whose valuation and future may inspire less confidence. Or the improvise can mean we put the stock on a watch list and wait to make a decision. Wait to see if the new management team can, in fact, deliver. Wait to see if the new designs take hold. We may pay a little more by waiting but we will likely reduce our potential downside risk. Finally, we can also improvise by selecting in which specific accounts to own the stock—matching up our life goals and the timing associated with each objective. For a shorter-term goal we may not want to own a stock whose valuation is less compelling like COH's. There may not be enough time for management to ultimately get things right before we need to fund a particular objective—the most obvious being a child's college education. But in our retirement account with a much longer time horizon we may be willing to take the incremental risk. This is the nuance, the judgment, the improvise, if you will, that allows us to express our confidence in a holding based on how the stock measures up to the factors we establish.

With our first case study, Apple Computer, the stock's valuation metrics are more conclusive and compelling than COH's. Though we have a relatively new management team at AAPL that team has turned a corner by successfully delivering new products and improved earnings growth. The stock (or the company for that matter) may not be out of the woods but they seem to have found the trail and are moving toward the clearing. And the stock price has appreciated some to reflect increasing investor confidence. For this reason Apple has the potential to become a core long-term holding in our portfolio. Coach, on the other hand, is earlier in the turnaround and has yet to produce positive, measurable results. Depending on your risk tolerance and investing goals, at this point COH—if owned at all—should reflect a much smaller holding until the company makes progress toward restoring its former luster.

Paying Attention to Your Selected News Sources Can Provide a Catalyst for Your Portfolio Decision

When a stock is stuck in the neglect stage of investor grief, the chatter goes quiet. No one really wants to talk about the stock; analysts don't want to go out on a limb and recommend it and the media takes little interest in a turnaround story until it turns around. Remember: Wall Street is a real-time tug-of-war between fear and greed. At the price bottoms, people are fearful; no one wants to make the first move. So when people begin talking about the stock take notice. Stock prices go up when there are more buyers than sellers; consequently positive chatter can create upward pressure to the price. And despite what people tell you at cocktail parties most lay investors often don't get into a stock until well after the smart money has made a tidy sum. Analyzing and reanalyzing our qualitative and quantitative factors, paying attention to the news, wandering through a Coach store and casually interviewing the clerks (I actually do this), noticing the bags on the arms of your friends, or on the arms of your daughter's friends will improve your timing and inform your portfolio decision in ways that will benefit long-term performance.

In December of 2013 *Barron's* wrote an article entitled, "Coach's New Bag of Tricks," suggesting that the stock could climb 25 percent in two years as the new CEO transforms the firm.[1] The article is worth reading if you are interested in considering a position in Coach for your portfolio, but one particular statistic caught my attention. Since going public in December of 2011, Michael Kors (KORS) has grown its market capitalization to 16.5 billion compared to Coach's market capitalization of 15.6 billion. In a matter of one to two years KORS has appreciated to a level in excess of the market value of the 72-year-old Coach. Despite the fact that COH is the share leader in the handbag industry, with 29 percent of the premium handbag market, it is valued at less than the relative upstart, Michael Kors. This comparison harkens back to our Google, Apple comparison in the previous chapter. In its short public history, KORS has not only exceeded the market value of Coach but demands a p/e premium trading at almost 29x 2014 earnings. Or close to double the p/e of COH. Though I am unwilling to draw conclusive determinations from such a short history, the numbers are illustrative of the market's willingness to pay a premium for growth leaders. Just as investors are willing to believe Google will grow at double the rate of Apple into the future they are also wagering that KORS will continue to generate growth double that of Coach. If, or when, Coach regains momentum, it is safe to assume that investors will once more be willing to pay a premium for the company. Watch for the indications that the stock is returning to favor by looking for positive news stories and positive indications among the consumers you know.

DON'T FORGET TO CONSIDER WHAT THE DIVIDEND IS TELLING YOU

Remember, too, the information we can glean from the dividend and the dividend policy established by the board and management team. Not only does the dividend provide us with insight into what management potentially believes about future earnings, it provides us with an upfront return. In the case of Coach, the stock is yielding 2.4 percent and the dividend has grown significantly in recent years. A quick review of the company's **10-K** (available online) revealed the following statement about the dividend initiated during the fiscal fourth quarter of 2009: "The Company initiated a cash dividend at an annual rate of **$0.30** per share. During the fourth quarter of fiscal 2010, the Company increased the cash dividend to an annual rate of **$0.60** per share. During the fourth quarter of fiscal 2011, the Company increased the cash dividend to an annual rate of **$0.90** per share. During the fourth quarter of fiscal 2012, the Company increased the cash dividend to an annual rate of **$1.20** per share. During the fourth quarter of fiscal 2013, the Company increased the cash dividend to an expected annual of **$1.35** per share." I include the report's bland repetition to emphasize the company's dividend growth history and the recent slowdown in that growth. Does the dividend growth reflect management's expectations for earnings growth in the future? Seems likely.

Just as we did with Apple, let's take a look at ETF alternatives that provide diversified exposure to Coach.

ETF Options For Those Who Want to Diversify Their Exposure to Coach

There are many ways to gain exposure to high-end purveyors of retail goods like Coach without taking on the specific stock risk. ETFs provide an excellent investment opportunity for investors to focus exposure to specific industries or capitalization ranges, global regions, and other portfolio diversifying strategies. For exposure to the consumer discretionary stocks (which is the industry category Coach falls into) I have selected the Vanguard Consumer Discretionary ETF (**ticker:** VCR) and the i-Shares Global Consumer Discretionary Stock ETF (**ticker:** RXI) for comparative purposes. Both contain exposure to COH. The VCR expense ratio is 0.14 percent versus the RXI, which charges 0.48 percent. When the price performance is looked at over time, the performance differential between the two funds is about equal to the fee differential. Vanguard's fund outperforms the RXI over the most recent two- and five-year period. Lower fees are almost always one

of the primary criteria I use when selecting an ETF because generally ETFs in the same industry track the same index and though
they may employ different methodologies (often the reason cited
for higher fees) the end result cannot be materially disparate. The
performance advantage often comes from lower fees.

Over the most recent two-year period Coach underperforms not
only the VCR and the RXI but also the S&P 500. As the stock fell
from grace and passed through the four stages of investor grief,
holders of COH were punished significantly. But when we compare
the performance of Coach versus the market and the two ETFs
over a five-year period we confront a very different picture. Coach
fares much better. Time usually smoothes out the extremes and
rewards specific stock risk versus the diversified returns of funds
(just as we saw with AAPL). Although the VCR is still the top performer (and by a good margin), Coach outperforms the RXI and
the S&P 500. Here again, the investment time horizon matters.
Goals-based investing means selecting the investment most likely
to generate superior returns during the period you are invested for
a specific goal. The shorter the time horizon the less specific stock
risk you will want to take as the two charts confirm. If we were to
look back even longer—say from the time Coach went public—
COH and the funds have dramatically outperformed the S&P 500
and we would have fared about comparably in the funds versus an
individual holding in Coach. In this case, the specific stock risk has
not produced nearly as much excess return as AAPL did relative
to the fund alternatives. You could certainly argue, however, that
owning COH stock versus one of the ETFs would have resulted in
much higher levels of volatility. Factor that into your investment
decision. Consider whether you have the time horizon and appetite
for risk to hold a such a stock. When considering COH versus the
funds versus simply being invested in the S&P 500 (via one of the
plethora of ETFs tracking the S&P) over varying time periods you
can reach very different conclusions as to which option is superior.
The market is dynamic—always changing, often confounding—
which is why you will want to consider your goals carefully against
the portfolio you construct. As much as I love holding individual

stocks, when my research is inconclusive as it is with COH I step to the sidelines. ETFs are an excellent and sometimes superior alternative. Particularly for life goals with a more immediate time horizon.

Intelligent Investing Rule #9: *Remember investing is an iterative process—we necessarily make adjustments as new information becomes available. Owning the stocks of industry leaders can provide significant excess return to the patient investor; however, there will be times when you will choose to diversify your risk by owning an ETF.*

Whichever investment vehicle you choose, remember the analogous comparisons we discussed at the beginning of the chapter. Investing is like many aspects of our lives. It is an iterative process because the information available to us changes and because the market is merely a collection of people with evolving desires and needs—a dynamic marketplace—that rewards patience. And informed courage. While your acquaintances spout off about the latest **initial public offering** darling remember to keep in mind *your* investment goals, *your* time horizon, *your* qualitative and valuation factors, and *your* investment discipline. Investing is as much about taking risks as it is about knowing your limitations. As much about patience as knowing when to draw the line. Investing requires many of the traits women exhibit on a daily basis: a steely yet flexible demeanor, a willingness to take a stand but remain open to compromise, to navigate tumultuous waters successfully, keeping an eye on the horizon, day in and day out.

CHAPTER 10

Stocks to Own for a Lifetime: Identifying Industry Leaders Provides the Conviction Required to Buy Stocks We Are Willing to Hold for Decades

I have asserted that investing is iterative; investing can also be inspired by literature. Author Annie Dillard in her book, *The Writing Life*, offers the following advice to those who wish to create on the page: "Write as if you were dying."[1] What if we invested the same way? If like the 80-year old bond scion whose portfolio was 100 percent allocated to stocks, we invested as though our time horizon were infinite? If we bought stocks to own for a lifetime and beyond? Stocks in companies that are durable, that will stand up to long-term scrutiny. If we own only the best stocks in each sector or industry—lifetime stocks—would they not also be suitable investments for achieving our financial goals?

To acquire the conviction needed to own stocks for a lifetime and beyond we must be sure (as we can be) that we are buying only the truly great, the survivors in an ever-changing world. In previous chapters we have identified important qualitative factors that must be evident in the companies of the stocks we want to own: great management team and corporate culture, brand and industry dominance, and innovation or adaptability. And we have identified important quantitative factors: the dividend as management's proxy for earnings growth, the p/e, the p/s ratio, and the price/earnings to growth ratio (PEG). We also examined two case studies against those factors: Apple, a stock that exhibits the characteristics of a core holding we could own for a lifetime, and Coach, a stock that does not yet meet our criteria. Though COH may ultimately have a place in a portfolio, given its ranking according to our factors we have to at least consider the notion that the company might not succeed or may even, at some point, be acquired. The jury is still out on Coach's recovery. Stocks to own for a lifetime must be survivors. Companies like Microsoft, IBM, and Intel may currently be on the wrong side of innovation but because of their sheer size and market dominance these leaders have pricing power, the ability to buy out smaller competitors, and superior management teams with the corporate culture to manage through difficulties. Survival is in their DNA. And that is what makes them candidates—like Apple—for our list of stocks to own for a lifetime.

Returning to my IBM versus the cashmere sweater example in the first chapter, we have seen it is true that great companies deliver performance over the long-term. It is also true that dominant brands like Apple, Disney, Starbucks, and Nike thrive despite short-term problems or the emergence of new competitors. Searching for the great and eschewing the mere good is the only way we can be assured our investments will produce excellent performance over our lifetime and the lifetimes of those that follow us. And owning stocks for a lifetime also suits the skills women inherently bring to the investment table: an interest in research, a desire to buy and hold, and instinctive good judgment. So, in the interest of diversification let's take a look at a few stocks—a portfolio of core holdings with representation from various economic sectors—that we can feel comfortable owning for a lifetime. In the following chapter we will consider four ETFs that can also be held for the long haul.

You Can't Beat the Real Thing: Coca-Cola, Consumer Staples Sector, Soft Drink Industry

Coca-Cola (**stock ticker: KO**) is the quintessential stock to own for a lifetime and represents one of my core holdings. I cannot say I personally consume a great deal of Coke products (nor did I encourage my kids to do so) but the company's global brand power is undeniable. As far as valuation, it is almost never the cheapest stock in my portfolio—though there have been times when the stock has fallen from grace and offered a compelling valuation. But for the most part I own Coke for the dividend yield, the stable growth and dominant market share, unparalleled brand recognition, and smart financial management. Oh yes, and its defensive characteristics. With a stable and growing yield this consumer staple stock exhibits defensive characteristics in a declining or flat market, though it sometimes lags in frothy, rising markets. Over the last 45 years (the longest period for which I could find data) through the end of 2013, the stock has returned 11.8 percent per year versus 9.9 percent for the S&P 500.

As I was doing research for this book I came across an article (again in *Barron's*) about one of the great investors: Fayez Sarofim. The subheading read: "The biggest lesson from Fayez Sarofim's five decades in the investment business: Buy Quality stocks...and hold them forever."[2] And the first stock mentioned in the article? "Brand behemoths" like Coca-Cola. But even more important, Sarofim, like Buffett and those of us who are interested in putting together a portfolio of investments for a lifetime understands that when we buy great companies we don't have to worry about when to get out—price declines are often opportunities to buy more shares at a bargain—relieving us of the worry of having to vigilantly watch over our holdings. And we don't have to worry about paying the big tax bills that come with active trading. Buying stocks for a lifetime is one of the most powerful, tax-efficient ways to create wealth.

BRAND DOMINANCE CREATES PRICING POWER

We place a great deal of emphasis on brand dominance—because it provides the company with pricing power. And pricing power contributes to the strength and sustainability of the earnings growth over the long haul—not just next year. The "dead money" crowd will often question the viability of a staid grower like KO, particularly after a year when Internet stocks catapult the index to new highs as they did in 2014. The criticism has happened before. It will happen again. Among other worries for these investors is the societal emphasis on reducing soda consumption and that allows the Coke naysayers to once more dominate the dialogue. The company's growth days are numbered, they claim. As they have claimed before. Yet, Coke is unlikely to fade away. Here's why.

Coca-Cola provides an excellent example of how stocks to own for a lifetime sustain and even thrive following difficult times. A growth stock that fell from grace due to an earnings miss almost forty years ago placed the venerable growth stock on the roster of Fallen Angel growth stocks of great companies. In the mid-seventies KO was the growth stock every manager loved to own. After decades of superior earnings growth the company ran into problems. The company's challenge began with rising sugar prices, which compressed earnings margins and caused the most momentum-oriented growth investors to sell. Coke stock had entered the first phase of investor grief: disappointment. Then container costs rose, further compressing margins and exacerbating investors. Frustrated, those investors sold, providing additional pressure on the stock price and for years it traded in a narrow and depressed range. Coke then passed into the second stage of investor grief: hate. Once the bad news snowballed, analysts suddenly began to question the ability of Coca-Cola to ever grow again. Studies were commenced and the results showed that KO's market share and earnings growth were unlikely to grow further. The studies theorized that soft drink consumption in the United States was so immense it was not possible for the human body to ingest increasing amounts without adverse health consequences and, therefore, the company was unlikely to grow at the rates previously attained. And just like that the stock passed into the third stage: neglect. There it languished while management attempted a diversification strategy that did little to solve the company's problems. What investors were really concerned about was growth in Coca-Cola's core business. And, since they were convinced the soft drink business would never grow again they saw no reason to hold the stock or buy the stock (no matter how cheap it was, and it was cheap!). While Coca-Cola wallowed in Wall Street neglect, savvy value investors were buying up the shares. They had a few years to do so (collecting a safe and robust dividend every quarter—in effect, getting paid to wait for things to improve) before management eventually righted the ship and started delivering compelling earnings growth, aided in large part by a factor totally overlooked by skeptical investors: growth in Europe. The subsequent fifteen years produced outstanding returns for those smart enough to get in when most investors were ignoring the stock. Here again we find that a bad stock of a good company is often a great investment. That's the historical perspective, now let's look at the company's current woes.

Coca-Cola has once more lost its fizz. Since the end of 2011 the stock has dramatically lagged the performance of the stock market. Analysts are forecasting a downshift in consumer soda consumption; add to that an economic slowdown in the most recent growth market for KO—emerging markets—and the pessimists on the stock are a dime a dozen. Yet, the company's global distribution network is unmatched and this management team is savvy enough to figure out how to leverage it. Management has been delivering earnings growth in the mid-single digits even during the global recession and the company continues to increase the dividend at an average rate of just over 8 percent per year, signaling that long-term, sustainable earnings growth is closer to 8 percent than the recent 4 percent.

Coca-Cola is the largest beverage company in the world, with distribution in over 200 countries, boasting 1.8 billion servings per day. KO's 500 brands generate over $47 billion in annual revenue but it is important to note that 16 of its brands generate over $1 billion each per year. In other words, brand dominance. The company has guided Wall Street to expect 3–4 percent in annual volume growth (beverages consumed), which will result in 5–6 percent in revenue growth (higher pricing due to flexibility as industry leader) and through sound financial management the company expects to generate "high single digit" earnings growth. That lines up nicely with the company's 8 percent historical dividend growth. Analysts cite a number of anecdotal reasons Coke's beverage consumption should reignite but the most compelling case for continued growth in KO is not dissimilar from another growth spark for the company over forty years ago: global markets. According to a 2011 study by global tax firm EY the middle class is expected to expand by three billion people by 2030. A growing middle class is traditionally good for Coke sales. And though governments are targeting sugary beverages—the Mexican government recently imposed a tax per liter—KO's industry dominance provides it with the pricing power to absorb the tax more easily than its competitors (Table 10.1).

Table 10.1 Coca-Cola financial factors vs. industry and S&P 500

Financial factors	Coca-Cola	Soft drink industry	S&P 500
Dividend yield	2.7%	2.7%	2.1%
Dividend growth	8.06%	9.4%	7.9%
Earnings growth (3–5-year estimate)	8.6%	7.5%	4.4%
P/E (forward 12 months)	19.0x	19.6x	15.5x

Even when undervalued Coke never seems extraordinarily cheap when measured by p/e. At current levels when compared to its peers the stock seems reasonably priced given its higher projected earnings growth in 2014. But the beauty of buying stocks for a lifetime is that you can buy and add to your holdings year in and year out. Buy more when the market shuns them and add more modestly to your holdings when the stock price seems rich. As your portfolio and your wealth grow you will continue to make modest tweaks to your holdings—adding to some, trimming others. It may be an annual event (as prescribed for the Dogs of the Dow approach) but presumably some of your stocks will perform better than others each year and you will want to add to some with new savings or trim others that may have performed so well they've grown to dominate your portfolio. These choices are yours and will be based on your specific time horizon and life goals, how you construct your portfolio, and the taxable or tax-exempt nature of the funds. When you buy stocks for a lifetime, it is like planting a garden. You trim and prune as you see fit depending on the kind of garden you are attempting to produce. But our confidence comes in knowing that these industry dominators will eventually bloom because of their financial strength acquired through industry leadership.

As your portfolio grows and you seek additional exposure in the consumer staples sector there are plenty of great companies to acquire. **Runners up?** Industry dominators Wal-Mart (**stock ticker:** WMT), Costco (**stock ticker:** COST), and Proctor & Gamble (**stock ticker:** PG) are good choices. McDonald's (**stock ticker:** MCD) and SBUX provide industry leading exposure to the consumer discretionary sector, which is a close cousin to consumer staples. Each would be reasonable additions to your "Stocks for a Lifetime" portfolio.

Floating on the Cloud with Oracle, Information Technology Sector, Software Industry

Oracle (**stock ticker:** ORCL) is a software company in transition. But this is not the first time the company has regrouped and repositioned itself. This latest opportunity came when Oracle's CEO Larry Ellison supposedly and famously referred to the term cloud computing as: "complete gibberish." But, as is often the case with the media, the quote was taken out of context. Ellison was objecting to the notion that suddenly everything was considered "cloud computing." To my taste, far more interesting was his comment in answer to a question about cloud computing: "the computer industry is the only industry that is more fashion driven than women's fashion." In other words, he went on to explain, the definitions being applied to "cloud computing" were simply new ways of explaining the way software was already being delivered. Still, Oracle's stock price suffered as analysts fretted over the company's supposed lack of offerings in the "cloud." But Ellison also said that if the market wanted "cloud" he would give them "cloud." And since he has done so, the stock has appreciated over 30 percent.

Industry Leaders Can Solve Growth Problems through Acquisitions Thanks to Lots of Free Cash Flow

Oracle is the world's largest provider of enterprise software and now also characterizes itself as a leading provider of computer hardware products and "services that are engineered to work together in the *cloud* and in the data center" (emphasis mine). The company produced $37.1 billion in revenue growth in 2013 and $14 billion in free cash flow. Free of accounting gimmickry, free cash flow reveals the firm's financial strength to fund future growth and increase shareholder value through share repurchases and dividend increases. Free cash flow is similar to what we have left over each month after paying all our expenses, and strong, free cash flow signals to investors the company's financial flexibility in funding growth organically or making strategic acquisitions. Free cash flow also signals an ability to increase shareholder return through dividends and share repurchases. In a June 2013 article published in *Barron's* entitled, "Six Stocks That Could Double in Five Years," Jack Hough notes that ORCL had recently doubled the dividend and in the previous year spent the equivalent of 8 percent of its current market value on share repurchases.[3] More recently, in December of 2013 Oracle announced the acquisition of Responsys Inc. (**stock ticker: MKTG**). The company specializes in "marketing automation," an area considered to be one of hyper growth in the cloud space. (Marketing automation is used by companies like Nordstrom and Southwest Airlines to tailor and track e-mail campaigns to customers.) If they want cloud, Ellison intends to give them cloud.

One of the most provocative CEO's in the country, Larry Ellison is not a man to bet against. He is also one of the smartest and most determined. In the last decade alone he has spent over $50 billion to buy 100 companies in strategic acquisitions—areas where Oracle's expertise needed plumping. He has deployed cash effectively in an effort to transform ORCL's underlying business as technology evolves. Industry leaders use their dominance not only to employ pricing flexibility but also to make strategic acquisitions in new growth areas of the market. And that is exactly what Ellison has done. His comments about the "cloud," while misinterpreted, didn't deter him from his objective to grow Oracle and to increase shareholder value. Following the Responsys acquisition and a good quarterly earnings report (after coming in shy of earnings estimates for an uncommon two quarters in a row) ORCL's stock has returned to a 13-year high. Yet, it is still reasonably priced (Table 10.2).

As you can see, ORCL's p/e is well below the industry average and below that of the S&P 500. The company also boasts an above market earnings growth estimate and a reasonable though below-market

Table 10.2 Oracle financial factors vs. industry and S&P 500

Financial factors	Oracle	Software industry	S&P 500
Dividend yield	1.3%	0.6%	2.1%
Dividend growth	75.0% (distorted by short dividend history)	30.2% (distorted by short dividend history)	7.9%
Earnings growth (3–5-year estimate)	16.5%	11.6%	4.4%
P/E (forward 12 months)	12.4x	32.4x	15.5x

yield. And despite the grousing from analysts and Oracle competitors that Ellison doesn't understand the "cloud," others (including
Bob Evans of *Forbes*) argue that "Oracle is the only tech company
on Earth that has a full product line at all levels of the cloud."[4] The
good news is that you don't have to guess who is right. What you do
know is that Oracle is a well-managed company with loads of cash;
a company that can solve innovation glitches through acquisitions
and a company that is relatively cheap compared to others in its own
industry. ORCL went public in 1986 (the return calculation is for the
period ending June 30, 1986–December 31, 2013), the stock is up
25.6 percent annually versus 10.0 percent for the S&P 500. In August
of 2013, as the naysayer volume rose I wrote in my blog: "Oracle may
stumble in the near term, but if you have a three to five year time
horizon, it may be time to take a serious look at Oracle. With strong
free cash flow, a modest but growing dividend, a price/earnings ratio
well below that of the market and a CEO who has 'righted' his vision
on the all-important cloud space, Oracle should be able to soar once
more." And when it stumbles again you can be assured ORCL has
the cash to acquire the technology or products it lacks.

Runners up? IBM, Intel Corporation (**stock ticker:** INTC),
EMC Corporation (**stock ticker:** EMC), GOOGL, and AMZN are
each industry leaders. Through your own research you must determine if they meet your investment strategy objectives but each company provides a good place to begin your research. (Note: we have
already discussed another technology industry leader: AAPL.)

By Now You Are Getting the Idea

At this point, I am sure you are beginning to realize that investing
is accessible to you no matter how busy you are and no matter how
inexperienced you are. By now I trust you understand there is a
vast amount of data available to you, easy to access, and free. I hope
you are eager to begin implementing what you've learned about
yourself, about investing, and about the ways you can achieve your
financial goals—not just for you but for generations to follow. So
many of the successful investors I know or have worked with over
the span of my career started with nothing in terms of wealth and

little in terms of knowledge. What set them apart was their willingness to work hard, to save, and to invest. So many of us only engage in the first half of the equation. But, as we have learned, the activity that really matters over the long-term (if we want to acquire wealth, that is) is investing.

Many years ago I managed a small portfolio for a very successful and wealthy businessman in New York. He had made millions in his own country and when that wealth was confiscated by the government he found his way to the United States and made fivefold what he had before. He was gracious and kind, not a trace of bitterness, and he was generous but he was also focused on his goal: To make more of what he had. And because he was a millionaire a hundred times over, I will admit, I wondered if he didn't have enough to finally rest and enjoy the results of his labor. But as I came to know him, I came to understand the wisdom of his effort, the determination to keep tending to the growth of his assets. He did so because it was the responsible and prudent thing to do.

Mr. Z—as I liked to call him—had given me a very small portion of his wealth to "try me out" and he would call me every few weeks to check on the growth of his portfolio of stocks. At first I reported how his assets had performed against the market but he soon made it clear he couldn't care less about my benchmark. What he cared about was how much his portfolio had grown. If the market performed better than his portfolio but he was satisfied with his return then he hung up a happy man. His was a simple equation really: he had a goal for his assets, he understood the risk he was willing to take, and he expected a reasonable return. No shoot-for-the-moon stock picks or **hedge fund**-like investments for Mr. Z. He invested for the long haul. He was interested in owning great companies that would increase the family wealth for generations to come. He was a man who invested as if he were dying.

JOHNSON & JOHNSON, HEALTH-CARE SECTOR, PHARMACEUTICALS—A PURVEYOR OF ICONIC BRANDS CAN OVERCOME PRODUCT LIABILITY PROBLEMS, MORE THAN ONCE

Finding great companies in the consumer staples or technology sectors is relatively easy for most of us. We are all consumers, after all, so we recognize great brands and have personal knowledge of the retailers and restaurants we frequent, as well. We are all also users of technology to a greater or lesser extent so we at least have a working knowledge of the companies that operate in that sector. But health-care companies seem to be less familiar to us. Though we go to the doctor and take aspirin or cold remedies from time to time, most of us are remarkably unfamiliar with the underlying drug companies.

An easy way to inform ourselves is to examine the largest holdings in a collection of health-care ETFs. This information is readily available; I went to the Bloomberg and Yahoo! Finance sites and I reviewed the top ten holdings of the largest health-care ETFs. One name consistently appeared at the top of each fund's ten largest holdings: Johnson & Johnson (**stock ticker:** JNJ). As a dominant holding amongst health-care funds it is reasonable to conclude that JNJ is one of the industry leaders in health care; and from our personal consumption experience we know that the company's consumer brands are well-regarded household names: Bandaids, Listerine, Tylenol and Motrin, Visine, Splenda, and JNJ's staple baby powder and baby shampoo are brand leaders all. But the company is also dominant in medical devices and diagnostics as well as prescription products. (JNJ is one of a few companies that straddles economic sectors though it is officially categorized as a pharmaceutical company.) Now that we have identified this industry leader we can begin to familiarize ourselves with the company to determine if its stock is one to own for a lifetime.

Each of us will approach the research process somewhat differently. That is as it should be. For my part, I like to begin with a historical look at the stock's performance compared to the S&P 500. So, I head back to Yahoo! Finance. In the search bar I type in JNJ (the stock's ticker) and then in the left margin I click on "Basic Chart" and up comes the one-year performance chart for JNJ. But one year is not enough perspective for me. So, I customize. In the section entitled "range" I click on "max." This provides me with the longest available stock price history for JNJ. Then I click in the box next to the S&P 500 so I will be able to compare JNJ's performance against that of the market. When I do so I see that JNJ has significantly outperformed the stock market over multiple decades. This is comparable to what we see from most industry leaders. Stable, consistent outperformance over the long-term. Since December 31, 1977 (the earliest period for which the data is available) through December 31, 2013 the stock has returned 14.4 percent annually versus 11.8 percent for the S&P 500 (Figure 10.1).

Next I consider shorter periods, again comparing the stock to the S&P 500. From the shorter periods, I acquire a different perspective. I can see that there are periods of time when the stock has underperformed the market but that is to be expected. Entirely normal. What I can also detect from the chart is the volatility of the stock or how widely the price swings. And with Johnson & Johnson there are no heart-stopping moves. The stock goes up and down to be sure but not with reckless abandon. And JNJ's long-term outperformance is particularly remarkable given the company's past product liability woes. Most specifically with Tylenol.

A 2002 article in *The New York Times* recounts the 1982 Tylenol tragedy that killed seven people in Chicago.[5] These individuals unwittingly took cyanide-laced capsules of Tylenol Extra-Strength. The bottles had been criminally tampered with, but nonetheless the public was likely to place the blame on JNJ's shoulders. The company demonstrated superior management and character when they immediately recalled 31 million bottles from store shelves and offered replacement medication free of charge. Their efforts recalling and relaunching Tylenol cost over $100 million but within two months JNJ returned the product to market in triple-tamper-proof packaging (a standard today but nonexistent prior to the Tylenol debacle). According to *The New York Times*, "A year later, its share of the $1.2 billion analgesic market, which had plunged to 7 percent from 37 percent following the poisoning, had climbed back to 30 percent." That is what superior management does. They manage through difficulties.

Of course today's management team will necessarily be comprised of different people but the company culture remains. And so do the problems, by the way. There have been additional recalls of Tylenol and lawsuits surrounding some of the company's artificial hips. But current CEO, Alex Gorsky is a twenty-one-year veteran

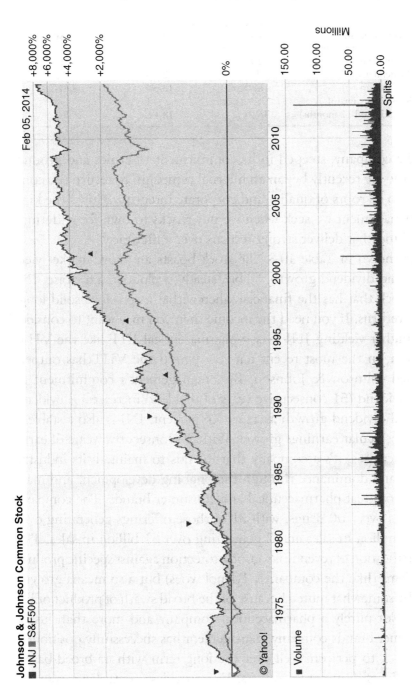

Figure 10.1 Yahoo! Finance historical price chart for Johnson & Johnson (JNJ). Reproduced with permission of Yahoo. ©2014 Yahoo. YAHOO! and the YAHOO! logo are registered trademarks of Yahoo.

Table 10.3　Johnson & Johnson financial factors vs. industry and S&P 500

Financial factors	Johnson & Johnson	Pharmaceutical industry	S&P 500
Dividend yield	2.8%	1.1%	2.1%
Dividend growth	7.6%	2.9%	7.9%
Earnings growth (3–5-year estimate)	6.9%	13.5%	4.4%
P/E (forward 12 months)	16.2x	18.4x	15.5x

of the company, steeped in its commitment to ethics and product quality. He recently began an internal campaign to return the company to its roots of quality and corporate integrity. This is the kind of management we seek when we buy stocks to own for a lifetime. The kind that deliver strong returns over a lifetime.

As shown in Table 10.3, the stock boasts an above-market yield and solid dividend growth. Stable, steady; a plodder, a tortoise, JNJ is a stock that has the financial wherewithal to produce solid long-term returns. If you need the income then you may want to consider the higher yielding JNJ over a pharmaceutical ETF like the VHT, though, in the most recent ten-year period the VHT has outperformed Johnson & Johnson. But, management's commitment to the dividend (51 consecutive years of dividend increases) is evident. Annual dividend growth averages 7.6 percent. JNJ is also a stable if not spectacular earnings grower. With 29 consecutive years of earnings increases, it's a company that intends to maintain its industry and brand dominance through the ongoing development and marketing of great pharmaceutical and consumer brands. The company markets over 100 drugs, with 31 of those offerings generating over $100 million in sales and 7 generating over $1 billion in sales. The diversification of revenue is a good protection against specific product problems (like the company's Tylenol woes) but also means growth will be somewhat muted because of the broad swath of product offerings. Not purely a pharmaceutical company and more than just a consumer brands company, management has successfully positioned the stock to perform well over the long-term with its broad-based portfolio of dominant products. JNJ provides an excellent example of a company that has faced product liability problems and dealt with them successfully all the while still growing company earnings and dividends. As investors we should be prepared to accept some risk but if we own the right stocks with the right management team we can expect long-term, even a lifetime of solid performance and income growth.

Runners Up? Merck & Co., Incorporated (**stock ticker:** MRK), Abbott Laboratories (**stock ticker:** ABT), Pfizer Incorporated (**stock ticker:** PFE), Amgen Incorporated (**stock ticker:** AMGN), and Gilead Sciences Incorporated (**stock ticker:** GILD). Again, which stocks you choose to add over time depends upon you and your risk and return expectations and valuation criteria.

Intelligent Investing Rule #10: *Stocks to own for a lifetime should be the stocks of great companies that are industry and brand leaders with a track record of sound, ethical management. The survivors, who dominate their industry. Build a portfolio of these great companies across economic sectors for your lifetime holdings.*

FINDING STOCKS TO OWN FOR A LIFETIME IS NO MYSTERY; IT SIMPLY TAKES A WILLINGNESS TO DIG A LITTLE AND LEARN A LOT

The market is divided into ten economic sectors and numerous industries within each sector. Consequently there are plenty of opportunities for you to find industry leading candidates for your portfolio of stocks to own for a lifetime while still diversifying across economic sectors. Which stocks you choose will depend again on your research and your personal biases. For example, in the financial sector you may find that a dominant global financial services firm like JPMorgan Chase (**stock ticker:** JPM) is far too complicated and engaged in far too many businesses and geographic regions for you to develop a clear understanding of the company. However, you might find a company like American Express (**stock ticker:** AXP) accessible and easy to understand. Or, perhaps, Visa (**stock ticker:** V) or MasterCard (**stock ticker:** MA), all credit card companies with a clear and focused business. Maybe you bank at Wells Fargo (**stock ticker:** WFC) and decide this industry leader is a stock you would like to own. Within the financial sector there are a number of industries but the primary ones are, broadly: insurance, banks, consumer finance, asset managers, and real estate investment trusts. By following the approach we established for JNJ you can search the ETF sector funds for the industry leaders and determine if there is a stock among those holdings that you can own for a lifetime. Or, just as with Apple and Coca-Cola you may decide to select a stock based on your personal knowledge of the company.

The same process can be followed for industrials and energy companies. I don't find either space particularly interesting but I understand the need to gain exposure to each sector and so I do so with stocks I can own for a lifetime in my long-term account. Stocks like Caterpillar Tractor (**stock ticker: CAT**), a global leader in industrial equipment that has paid a dividend every year since 1925 when the company was formed; 3M Company (**stock ticker: MMM**), an economic bellwether that manufacturers about 50,000 products from Scotch tape and Post-it Notes (how would we live without either!) to stethoscopes and aerospace adhesives; or Chevron Corporation (**stock ticker: CVX**), a multinational energy company, to name a few. In accounts with a shorter time horizon I will often purchase an ETF to avoid specific stock risk while still gaining exposure to each sector.

NOT EVERY STOCK IN YOUR PORTFOLIO HAS TO WORK OVER EVERY TIME PERIOD

Remember the five-stock portfolio I discussed in chapter 6. Five stocks diversified across five economic sectors measured over ten years. All stocks one could potentially feel comfortable owning for a lifetime. Yet only two of them outperformed the market—though dramatically—during the period measured. Three underperformed and one of the three underperformed significantly. Still, the portfolio of five stocks beat the market by about 150 percent cumulatively. That is why we own more than one stock. Despite our very best efforts we can't predict which stock will outperform during a specific period. In an interview given to *Barron's* in January of 2014, Kenneth French, professor of economics at Dartmouth (the French of Fama-French capital-asset pricing model fame), opined that if investors were given one day or one hundred years to establish an expected return for a particular stock they would be more accurate in determining the return after one hundred years.[6] Time and observation lend perspective. The worst performing stock of my five-stock portfolio was Citigroup and based on its growth and earnings prospects at this point I would be inclined to hold onto it. Though a colossal disappointment C has made many of the important adjustments to eventually secure better relative performance from current levels and into the future. General Electric, the second worst performing stock in my 2003 five-stock portfolio, has a similar profile. At this point, reversion to the mean and analysis of the financial and qualitative factors would argue for continuing to hold these two stocks. Not to mention Intelligent Investing Rule #1, which argues that having any investment discipline is better than no discipline at all. And further argues that once we establish a discipline we should not deviate. If Citigroup and GE still meet my investment criteria I should stick with them. And, for the most part, they do.

Sometimes I see my portfolio of stocks much the same way I see my friends. None is like the other. Rarely are they all up, or in the case of friends, upbeat at the same time. One particular friend is always there when I need her, another is more elusive but engaging and charming when we do get together. One friend provides intellectual stimulus, while another just makes me laugh. Each has a purpose and each holds me up in a different way at different times; each provides different benefits.

So when I encounter a stock like Cisco (also a member of my five-stock portfolio), with a management that has failed for over a decade to deliver on its promises I think of that friend (we've all had one) who never quite participates fully in the friendship contract. Who takes but doesn't give and who never holds herself accountable. And I wonder if it is time to cut the cord or if I should hang on just a little longer.

REMAIN DISPASSIONATE BUT DILIGENT—HOW TO CONSIDER WHEN TO PUNT

Is ten years long enough to wait for a company management to deliver? Cisco Systems is a former go-go growth company with a dominant product and marketing franchise whose prospect for organic growth has slowed. CSCO is now being priced by the market as a mature company. However, that doesn't mean the company isn't generating gobs of cash. Indeed, it is. In recent years the board initiated a dividend and for the moment it looks like a traditional value stock.

CSCO was one of the tech darlings of the 1990s, rising a cumulative 69,230 percent from its public offering in February of 1990 through December 31, 1999. That equates to a 94 percent annual return compared to 25.6 percent for the NASDAQ over the same period. Then, as though on cue, at the dawn of the twenty-first century, the stock stalled out, tail-spun into a rapid descent, and, finally, flatlined with little hope (or expectation) of robust future earnings growth or stock price outperformance. For the following decade the stock returned a negative single digit return as it made its adjustment from growth darling to value exile. The company cut costs, made acquisitions in new technologies, and Cisco management and the board of directors initiated a dividend in 2011. Since then the quarterly dividend has gone up three-fold, resulting in an expected yield of about 2.8 percent.

When rocket-propelled growth stocks mature, the initiation of a dividend is often perceived by investors as a declaration of surrender to future growth opportunities for the company. But, as we have discussed, the dividend can signal what management and the board think about future earnings growth. CEO John Chambers said as much about a recent dividend increase in August of 2012: "We wanted to send a message to shareholders." Slowing growth does not necessarily have to be a death knell for future stock price performance. Nor does the initiation of a dividend. The market is full of many companies that have successfully made the transition from growth to value stock and have gone on to generate solid performance. International Business Machines, like CSCO, managed the growth maturation process and also dealt with the additional burden of shifting technological trends.

After maturing from Nifty-Fifty growth stock darling to mature, old-fashioned computer company, IBM spent a decade in exile just as Cisco did. But the company transformed its underlying business from mainframe-dependent to personal computer-driven in the early 1980s and eventually earnings growth as well as the stock price reaccelerated. Then PCs took a backseat to laptops and IBM again made the adjustment. By the time the iPhone and iPad challenged traditional laptop computing, IBM had already transformed itself into a cloud-centric, services-driven technology company. Since January 30, 1968 (the earliest data I could find) through May 31, 2013—including all the company's fits and starts—IBM has provided a total return of 3,483.08 percent (including reinvestment of the dividend) or 8.2 percent per year. Transitions orchestrated by great managements can occur. But in order to do so management must deliver. In 1982 in the face of slowing soft-drink sales Coke management engineered a failed diversification plan when they bought Columbia Pictures but then regrouped and redoubled efforts to grow KO's core business, eventually shedding the motion-picture unit. Oracle management made acquisitions to round out their cloud offerings when they encountered competition and began losing share in their traditional applications business and JNJ has aggressively and wisely handled product liability problems. Great companies effectively manage transitions.

CSCO must demonstrate the same kind of transition leadership. Investors have generally been willing to give CEO John Chambers the benefit of the doubt. Though analysts rarely agree on the future prospects for CSCO most have been willing to concede Chambers' excellent leadership. If anyone could navigate the company back to growth it was Chambers. Until recently. Until yet another earnings miss and explanations from the CEO that disappointed. After a decade of underperformance investors are irritable and tired and the chorus is declaring the stock is cheap for good reason, that management is no longer up to the job. I'm tired, too. I want to sell the stock if only so I don't have to be reminded of what a disappointment it has been. Ironic? Yes, it has performed better than Citigroup and General Electric, the two stocks I said I would likely keep in my five-stock portfolio. But remember that the market builds on expectations. Predictability is prized. Cisco is that unreliable friend who promises to pick you up at 7:00 and never shows but then is early to pick you up the next time and offers to pay for dinner. Cisco is the perfidious pal, the inconsistent one you can never count on. And that makes it almost impossible for investors to estimate future earnings growth and, therefore, what the price target for the stock should be.

There are mitigating factors, of course: we have a robust dividend that has been growing at a healthy clip, we have a board and management committed to paying out half of free cash flow to shareholders in the form of dividends and share buybacks, and we have a CEO just years from retirement who would much rather leave a legacy of growth than lethargy. Even if the company never returns to above-market growth with a strong and growing dividend and earnings growth in the single digits it can likely limp along with market-level returns. The last ten years CSCO has generated positive returns—approximately 5 percent annually—and although 2.5 percent per year below the market's return it beats what I could have earned on my money elsewhere and moves me closer to my financial goals. So, I remain dispassionate, but diligent. I am not selling my shares but as I add to my savings I am not adding to my shares either. I own enough; I'm in it for the long haul but until I see a glimmer of consistency from this management team I am going to dilute my exposure by not adding to my holdings as my overall assets grow.

It's like keeping that flakey friend on the invite list for a big party but avoiding intimate exposure to her lest she disappoint once more. In a crowd, her behavior is muted and in her case that is a good thing. If our other lifetime stocks are any guide, CSCO shareholders are likely to receive a decent return, boosted somewhat by a generous dividend and relatively low levels of volatility. I will ignore my emotions and my ego and hold on a little longer. Like Mr. Z, I will focus on what I've gained rather than what I might have gained. For just a little while longer.

CHAPTER 11

ETFs to Own for a Lifetime: How Women Investors Can Get Their Groove Back

In my senior year of college I needed three physical education units to graduate. The only class that suited my schedule was Beginning Golf, so first thing every Tuesday and Thursday morning I arrived at the municipal course for an hour of anguish on the driving range. Our instructor walked down the line offering praise and tips to each student until he encountered me strategically tucked on the very last mat. Here he spent a good portion of the rest of the class explaining, re-explaining, instructing, deriding, demonstrating, reminding, encouraging, and finally, in desperation, yelling. I was the one student in the class who pushed the teacher to his limit. Having never flunked a student he wasn't about to let me go down but I was giving him a run for his money. Each class session I would arrive with a blank slate of skills as though the previous lessons had never occurred. "Keep your head down," he reminded. And I would tuck my chin a little more. "Now dip your left shoulder. No! Not like that." And my stress radar would go off at an alarming rate as he lurched closer and reached over, grabbed each of my shoulders in his hands and sharply made the adjustment. "Now just a little bend of the knees, check your grip and swing." And just as I began my back swing, stiff and mechanical, he barked, "Would you just relax?"

I know for women who already operate at full capacity that investing can be as overwhelming as attempting golf was for me. Independently, the notions we have discussed in this book seem accessible, even doable, but somehow when we attempt to pull the whole activity together we feel bogged down, swamped. I could keep my eye on the ball just fine but when I had to combine that with bended knees and a dipped shoulder and a grip that felt as unnatural and uncomfortable as my first prom dress, I froze. I needed to develop my own rhythm, my own swing away from the penetrating gaze of my instructor. Not until I practiced and practiced—till the blisters popped on my unaccustomed palms— and the swing became second nature, did I begin to hit the ball. Not until the effort became part of my muscle memory, like walking and sitting and riding a bike, did I marginally succeed in the sport. The same is true for investing. For those who do not yet have an interest in owning individual stocks—because you haven't yet mastered your investing swing—we will consider four ETFs that provide diversification, low costs, and very low portfolio turnover. These funds will be an excellent place to park your assets until you get your own unique swing down, until investing becomes natural and a permanent component of your muscle memory.

THE VANGUARD S&P 500 ETF (VOO)—COST-EFFECTIVE EXPOSURE TO THE BROAD MARKET

The ETF industry turned twenty years old in 2013 and since its inception has captured over $1.5 trillion in assets representing just under 10 percent of all mutual fund assets. In 2013 alone $188.5 billion flowed into ETFs, topping the $188.4 billion invested in 2012 according to *The Wall Street Journal.* From 2000 to 2010 the industry grew 30 percent per year versus the mutual fund industry, which grew at 5–6 percent annually. According to some estimates ETF assets are expected to at least double over the next five years. Global management and consulting firm, McKinsey and Company, in a 2011 white paper entitled, "The Second Act Begins for ETFs" argues that ETFs have provided investors with "access to asset classes and strategies once out of reach," that ETFs have "democratized" access to investing.[1] If so that is excellent news for busy women.

The most prevalent funds are those that provide broad market exposure by tracking the S&P 500. There are plenty of S&P 500

ETFs on the market and they produce returns that line up almost precisely with the return on the S&P. I chose the VOO because it is the cheapest. S&P 500 ETFs are commodities and therefore price is the overriding characteristic we should focus on when we select one. The total annual expense ratio for the VOO is 0.05 percent or 5 basis points, which is the equivalent of five, one-hundreds of 1 percent. For each one-hundred dollars invested in the fund, the fee is five cents. I call that cost-effective. Another benefit of all S&P ETFs is their low portfolio turnover. The VOO generates a negligible 3 percent in turnover per year.

Investing in an ETF that tracks the index provides solid long-term returns. In chapter 2 we reviewed the work of Professor Jeremy Siegel of the Wharton School. His research shows that since 1871 the median return for stocks over every rolling 30-year period is 9.22 percent. Though his research does not specifically examine the S&P 500 (the index was created in 1923), Siegel examines the broad universe of stocks—a comparable universe to that which the S&P seeks to measure. So assuming that we can achieve something like the 9 percent long-term average by investing in the VOO, we can be confident in buying the fund particularly for accounts with a long time horizon (which is where I own it). The VOO, in short, provides diversified exposure to the stock market.

The one caution to index investing is that you will receive not only the same return as the market but also the same level of volatility as the market. This means that when the S&P 500 rises and falls your account will rise and fall accordingly. We know from the research conducted by Fama and French and discussed in chapter 3 that value-oriented stocks tend to outperform growth stocks by a wide margin over time. Value stocks also tend to exhibit lower levels of volatility than the overall market. They may go up less during frothy market periods but they also tend to go down less in extended market declines. We will consider a more value-oriented ETF later in the chapter but it is important to realize that investing in the VOO will produce returns comparable to the S&P 500 and volatility that will match the S&P 500. At about 9 percent per year over the long-term we can tolerate volatility

Because that is the kind of return that will grow our assets materially over a lifetime.

THE POWERSHARES QQQ (QQQ)—A MORE GROWTH-ORIENTED WAY TO TRACK THE MARKET

In the second half of 2013 we were told that the **smart money** was rotating out of defensive and interest-rate-sensitive stocks because of the worry over rising interest rates and relatively full valuations. The experts were clamoring for investors to place their money in more cyclical and growth-oriented names like those held in the QQQs. I have owned the QQQs for years – for me the fund is a lifetime holding because I want diversified exposure to the NASDAQ 100 stocks the ETF tracks. Because I also own individually some of the fund's top holdings I am mindful of and monitor my overall exposure to make sure I am not unwittingly exposed to too much of one holding. But many of the stocks in the biotech and technology space I would not have the expertise to research and it is this specialized exposure that attracts me to the QQQs. And the fee. It is higher than a pure index fund like the VOO but most certainly not expensive. The total annual expense ratio for the QQQ is 0.20 percent, 2/10's of 1 percent or 20 basis points, the equivalent of 20 cents for every $100 invested.

The top five holdings of the QQQs as of the end of 2013 were Apple at almost 12 percent of the fund, Google at just under 8 percent, Microsoft at 7.5 percent, Amazon at approximately 4.5 percent, and Intel at a little over 3 percent. But the fund includes more than just information technology stocks, which account for 56.5 percent of holdings. Biotechnology and medical equipment companies form about 14 percent of the fund and consumer discretionary comprises about 21 percent of the total fund assets. Knowing the weightings and the top five holdings can prevent you from overlap if you do, in fact, own individual stocks in your portfolio as I do. I occasionally review the fund's top holdings against my own holdings. If our Apple case study resonated with you but you don't want to take the specific stock exposure to Apple you can gain diversified ownership in AAPL by buying The QQQs.

But, if you did buy Apple, and decide you may want to own the QQQs as well you should keep in mind that in doing so you will have an incrementally larger percentage of your portfolio exposed to AAPL.

The QQQs have outperformed the S&P 500 over the long-term as we might expect but have also underperformed during shorter time horizons. With a more growthy bent, the index should experience greater volatility than the S&P 500 (the historical price chart comparing the two shows just this). Like the VOO the turnover is also extraordinarily low at 6.6 percent. Compare this against the average mutual fund, which turns over about 100 percent per year and you can see the after-tax benefits of owning ETFs over mutual funds. Additionally, it is important for us to note that for the trailing one-year period ending June 30, 2013, 59.6 percent of active large-cap mutual funds underperformed the S&P 500 according to S&P's director of research, Aye Soe.[2] Ms. Soe's research paints an even bleaker picture over the long-term. Fully 85.95 percent of large mutual funds underperform the index over three years and 79.5 percent underperform for the five-year period. When active mutual fund performance is also then considered, owning ETFs like the VOO and QQQs becomes even more compelling.

A Word about High Fees—the Wealth-Accumulating Woman's Enemy Number One

I was an active manager for my entire career. I like to believe in the notion that sound stock selection and a focus on value will beat the market over the long-term. And for many if not most of the years I managed money and mutual funds, I did just that. But not always and not with a guarantee. Mutual fund and investment advisor fees can run anywhere from 0.5 percent to upwards of 1.5 percent and those fees take an enormous toll on an investor's total return, particularly when compounded over many years. We have already seen the erosive effects fees can have on our retirement account in a previous chapter. But it is worth reviewing again that the level of fees is actually much higher than the average range indicates. Consider that your investment manager charges his fee on the total amount of assets you give him to manage. But you earned that money; it's yours; you own it. However, your manager is basing his fee on the assets you provided him. It would be more appropriate if the fee were charged against the assets the advisor produced or earned for you. Revisiting Charles Ellis' article, "Investment Management Fees Are (Much) Higher Than You Think," fees are "typically over 12% for individuals" when applied against the returns the manager produces. That should get your attention.

The research results consistently point to the same conclusion when it comes to investment fees. Higher fees erode total return. Nobel prize winner William Sharpe reminds us that investors who choose low-cost investments could end up with a 20 percent higher standard of living in retirement and Russel Kinnel of Morningstar claims that over every time period tested lower-cost funds beat high-cost funds. The results are overwhelmingly consistent: high fees are enemy number one. The legendary woman golfer, Nancy Lopez, once said, "The simpler I keep things, the better I play." The same is true of investment fees. Just remember: lower is always better.

Intelligent Investing Rule #11: *High investment management fees are Enemy #1 for women seeking to accumulate wealth. Remember fees are the single biggest threat to total return in your portfolio.*

THE VANGUARD DIVIDEND APPRECIATION ETF (VIG)— AN ETF WITH EXPOSURE TO VALUE-ORIENTED STOCKS WITH GROWING DIVIDENDS

The VIG focuses on companies with a history of growing dividends by tracking the US Dividend Achievers Select Index (a NASDAQ index). The fund produces a yield of around 2 percent and counts among its top ten holdings some of the premier large-cap companies in the world. Brand and industry dominators round out the top ten list—the kinds of survivor companies we have been focused on in this book. Companies like Abbott Labs, Coca-Cola, Proctor & Gamble, Pepsi, Wal-Mart Stores, McDonald's, 3M, and Chevron to name a few, and the top ten holdings represent 36 percent of the total fund. Here again the annual fee is nominal at 0.10 percent or

10 cents for every $100 invested. The turnover, though higher than the VOO and the QQQs, still comes in at a benign 15 percent. (As a professional investment manager my portfolio turnover was between 20 and 25 percent and that ranked me, in terms of turnover, in the lowest quartile of money managers measured.)

Since the fund's inception over five years ago the performance has exceeded that of the S&P 500—declining less in 2008 and generally keeping up in the subsequent **bull market** from mid-2009 to the end of 2013. The fund demonstrates the characteristics of all index funds (close tracking to the relevant index) but in the case of the VIG, the index tracked is more value-oriented and less volatile than the overall market. The VIG is a holding in my accounts where I am interested in having access to income and diversified exposure to the value segment of the market. An excellent fund for the long- and medium-term.

The iShares Core S&P Small Cap ETF (IJR)— an Excellent Way to Gain Exposure to Small-Cap Stocks

If we were to consult additional research from our friends Dr. Fama and Dr. French we would find that not only do value stocks tend to outperform over time but so do small-capitalization stocks. When possible, exposure to the small stock segment is a good way to add diversification and total return to your portfolio. Because of the specialized and focused nature of the research required to buy small companies I have historically left the management of my allocation and my client's allocation to the experts. In fact, if there were not such an abundance of reasonably priced small-cap ETFs available to individual investors, I would be inclined to agree it is worth paying a mutual fund management fee to gain access. But, there are plenty of ETF options available to investors and the one I like is the IJR. The fund does not charge a hefty fee, the total annual expense ratio is only 0.17 percent, and the annual turnover only 12 percent.

The IJR tracks the S&P 600 index that measures the performance of the small-capitalization sector of the US equity market. The IJR has an over ten-year history and I have owned it in all my accounts for at least half a dozen years. Because the fund has appreciated so significantly in recent years I have trimmed back my holdings to my target level for small-cap but I still own the fund and imagine I will for a very long time.

ETFs Are an Inexpensive Way for Women to Achieve Broad Diversification in the Market

All of the evidence directs us to the stock market for long-term total return. But, some are still hesitant to select individual stocks. I understand that fear. The finality and visibility of buying individual stocks can psyche us out. The same choking feeling I get when I have to hit a golf ball over the water. Intellectually I understand that hitting a ball over a water hazard is no different than hitting a ball over grass. I employ the same (awful) swing and presumably the ball flies the same (pathetic) distance. But for whatever reason, the water throws me. Just as individual stocks throw some women investors. Better to pick up my ball and set it in the fairway or camouflage my investment decisions in a diversified ETF. It may take me a few more strokes or a little longer but I still get where I am going. And in the end, that is the only thing that matters.

CHAPTER 12

Five Critical Lessons and Warnings: Don't Touch a Hot Stove, Don't Talk to Strangers, and Other Lessons for the Ages

As with most things in life you will quickly acquire your own investing experiences, both good and bad. And you will likely develop your own lessons and warnings; perhaps a list of "dos and don'ts," or "never agains," or even "next time I'll try." That is as it should be. But, for now start with the lessons and warnings in this chapter. Modify them as you see fit, add your own, and remain firm in your determination to avoid as many investing pitfalls as possible. It is much wiser to exercise caution in your investments, to get on base with singles and doubles rather than to swing for the fences. Smart women take informed risk. Doing so increases the odds we will keep out of trouble, avoid big losses, and protect our hard-earned and carefully saved money. Our Intelligent Investing Rules will keep us focused. These warnings will keep us out of the weeds.

IF YOU ARE DEPENDING ON THE DIVIDEND FOR INCOME AND VALUATION INFORMATION, MAKE SURE IT'S NOT TOO HOT NOR TOO COLD, BUT JUST RIGHT

It is first and foremost important that we understand the power of the dividend as a component of total return. As is often the case, we need to be wary of too much of a good thing. Since yield is good could a really high yield be even better? Not necessarily, as the research has shown. If life has taught me anything, moderation certainly is at the top of the list. Years ago my dermatologist prescribed Retin A for my skin. I figured if a morning dose was good, a morning and evening dose would be twice as good. Wrong. Two weeks and a cortizone shot later, the scaly red bumps—my skin's reaction to the Retin A overdose—finally disappeared. Painful lesson learned. The same is true of dividends. Too much of a good thing can sometimes be a signal of pending disaster.

There was a time not all that long ago when dividends didn't rise with the surety of a helium balloon on the end of a loose string. Because earnings were lethargic, dividend payments stagnated as well. That is as it should be. But when earnings are lethargic and the dividend continues to rise we need to become suspicious; the dividend should not increase faster than sustainable earnings levels for an extended period of time. We should also become suspicious when a dividend payout has reached a level that is no longer supported by earnings. We measure this by calculating the **payout ratio**. The payout ratio is simply the annual dividend payment divided by the annual earnings. Each company will determine the proper ratio based on their business and future earnings prospects. But when a company's payout ratio approaches or exceeds 100 percent of earnings we can be sure there is risk of a dividend cut. In 2013 the telecommunications services sector had a payout ratio of 151.2 percent (which means the companies in the sector were paying out 50 percent more in dividends than their earnings—certainly not sustainable),while the payout ratio for the S&P 500 was closer to 30 percent. High payout ratios can mean dividend risk and when the dividend is at risk we lose our rudder and a good portion of our total return. Bank stocks in 2009 were forced to cut dividends; auto companies are notorious cutters because of their cyclical earnings. The same is true for airlines. Be wary. A high relative yield is a positive—think Heartland's quintile 4—but a very high yield can carry risk, which is one of the reasons why the stocks in Heartland's fifth quintile underperformed.

In recent years as company management teams have improved their balance sheets and increased free cash flow (by living within their means), the opportunity to provide a return to their shareholders via the dividend has increased. As of the end of 2013, "the number of stocks paying dividends in the S&P 500 reached a 17 year high," according to the FACTSET Dividend Quarterly.[1]

Four hundred and seventeen companies in the S&P pay a dividend. That is 84 percent of the companies comprising the index. In the third quarter of 2013 alone companies paid out $84.4 billion in dividends. And $339.3 billion in the trailing twelve months. That amount is more than double the level of dividends paid out ten years prior. And 13 percent higher than the previous twelve-month period. Not surprisingly, company payout ratios at 31.5 percent are among the highest (non-recession) levels in ten years. That is good news for investors' pockets but why else is this information important? Robert D. Arnott and Clifford S. Asness published a 2003 research article entitled, "Surprise! Higher Dividends = Higher Earnings Growth," which concluded, "evidence strongly suggests that expected future earnings growth is faster when current payout ratios are high and slowest when payout ratios are low."[2] Historically investors assumed low payout ratios forecasted strong future earnings growth as management reinvested earnings into growth initiatives. But, in fact, what Arnott and Asness have concluded (supported by the data) is that within a reasonable payout ratio range of, say, 25–30 percent, these higher levels are forecasting stronger future earnings growth. (Note that for Arnott and Asness' purpose "high" is considered well below the abnormally high payout levels currently maintained by the telecommunications services sector and more in line with the current average payout of stocks in the S&P 500 at 31.5 percent). Further confirmation of the power of dividends as a valuation tool. Because of its importance to value investors we want to make sure that when we buy a stock for the dividend income and valuation information that the dividend is safe and reliable—not too high, not too low—and we do this by considering the sustainability of the dividend when compared to earnings via the payout ratio.

Don't Talk to Strangers; Taking Stock Tips From People Whose Investing Prowess Is Unknown To You Is Like Gambling

My high-school US government teacher had a policy that students could take every test three times and keep the highest score. His experience showed that rarely, if ever, did a student do better on the second or third try. And he told us that. Still almost every student tried their hand at taking the test three times, including me. When I did manage to eke out a good grade after the third effort it was sheer luck that propelled me. The same is true for investing. If, by chance, you buy a stock in which you have no knowledge or have not done the research and you succeed you will have learned nothing of value and may wrongly conclude you can repeat the serendipitous success. Buying a stock without knowing anything about the underlying company usually doesn't turn out very well. I know because I had to learn this lesson the hard way.

Many years ago on a flight from San Francisco to Houston, I met the charming CEO and CFO of a telecommunications company called SmartTalk. They had been touring the country touting their public offering of shares and were on their way home. By this point they had their pitch down pat. And I took the bait. Though they were perfect strangers to me, I didn't bother to do the research on their company and bought 100 shares each for my children's education accounts based solely on our airborne conversation. In less than two years, I watched the shares go from around $20 to zero: $4,000 of my hard-earned savings down the drain. But I didn't learn from that experience. Somehow it always takes more than once for me. A year later, a Swiss banker acquaintance fell over himself telling me about the latest biotech start-up stock he had purchased. Their drug was a sure thing and he had "made a great deal of money on stocks like this one." Again, I didn't bother to do the research and bought 500 shares on his enthusiastic recommendation. I was young and busy raising two kids, running a business and looking for a shortcut, so I rolled the dice and lost every penny. Five thousand dollars later I swore off others' great ideas forever.

Which is too bad because around ten years later in 2002, a prominent and highly successful money manager whose outstanding small-cap performance I was very well acquainted with, suggested—as a favor—I might want to take a look at Wynn Resorts (**stock ticker:** WYNN) for my IRA. He was impressed with the company's long-term growth potential and was buying the stock himself. But what did I know of gambling outfits? Or the hotel business for that matter? No, I wasn't going to fall for that again. Since his suggestion WYNN is up a cumulative 2,118.2 percent versus the S&P 500,'s 153.5 percent (through the end of 2013). If ever I was going to listen to a stock suggestion it should have been that one. I knew the performance and quality of the manager's work and could easily have supplemented his research with my own. But I didn't. I was under the influence of too small a sampling size based on my two previous failures. Still, despite the success of WYNN, to this day I won't buy a stock whose underlying business I don't know or understand. I will, however, put it on a watch list and do my own homework if the source of the idea is credible.

At least I finally learned the lesson.

Absolutely Do Not, Ever, Chase Stocks You Think You Should Have Bought and Didn't

I have been tempted to chase runaway stock prices as much as the next woman. WYNN is the perfect example. I look at it all the time wondering if now is a good entry point, bemoaning the fact that I "missed it." But, there will be plenty of opportunities in other stocks or, perhaps, once again in WYNN. What is key to achieving solid long-term performance is to stay the course—whichever course selected—and carry on. Trying to time a particular stock or the market is a fool's game for any investor but especially for busy women.

As an illustration let's consider some return data points for the Dow Jones Industrial Average in 1987. On October 19—Black Monday—the DJIA dropped 22.61 percent in one day. Had I panicked and sold I would have missed two of the top twenty largest one-day gains in the Dow since 1950. On the very next day, October 20, the index rose 5.9 percent and the following day, October 21, it rose another 10.2 percent. By selling I would have missed the partial bounce back and would have likely not reinvested to enjoy the next decade of stellar returns. Don't get me wrong. Black Monday was frightening. I was investing for clients in 1987 and I can still remember the panic as we all huddled around the trader's screen (back then we only had one "Quotron" that provided stock prices on the entire trading floor) and watched the DJIA plummet 508 points to 1,738.74. (It is instructive to note that the DJIA closed out 2013 at 16,576.70.) None of us knew what the following day would bring but we knew that over the long-term we were still interested in owning stocks. As Warren Buffett advises, "If you aren't willing to own a stock for 10 years, don't even think about owning it for 10 minutes." Being good value investors we stayed the course, added some to our holdings, and went on to enjoy one of the strongest bull market periods in history. Thankfully we didn't have to chase stocks or the market because we stayed in, we held on.

The table on the next page is instructive for women new to investing. When we look at market returns over the long-term and in context, we increase our sampling size and the odds that when stocks go south we will retain our conviction to remain invested. In our 24x7 news-cycle-world, negative news becomes magnified but if we maintain perspective (and historical returns provide perspective) we can increase our confidence that stocks will once more return to favor. Although today's investors focus on the recent difficult market in 2008 (which we will discuss below), note the three-year drag from 2000 to 2002. While the decline wasn't as drastic as 2008, the repeated negative performance year in and year out for three years took its toll on an earlier generation of investors. Again standing firm was the right thing to do. Look at what you would have subsequently missed if you bailed out during the 2000–2002 period (Table 12.1).

Using market weakness to add to holdings is a sound strategy. Simply buying and holding over the 27-year period (a reasonable time horizon for most of us) and including periods like Black Monday and 2000–2002 has resulted in significant appreciation—11.1% percent per year for 27 years. Applying the rule of 72s, my investment has doubled every six and a half years. If Jane Austen is right and "money is the best recipe for happiness," then investing in high-quality companies for the long-term, undeterred by market weakness, is a key ingredient.

But what if I wasn't born in 1987 or at the very least didn't have any investments? How about an event nearer and dearer to my heart, like 2008? Many investors are still trying to recover from the market decline of 2008. The memory is still all too vivid of a 401(k)

Table 12.1 Annual total return for Dow Jones Industrial Average, 1987–2013

Year	DJIA total return (including dividends)
1987	6.0%
1988	16.1%
1989	31.7%
1990	-0.6%
1991	24.3
1992	7.3%
1993	16.9%
1994	5.0%
1995	36.9%
1996	28.7%
1997	24.9%
1998	18.1%
1999	27.2%
2000	-4.8%
2001	-5.4%
2002	-15.0%
2003	28.3%
2004	5.3%
2005	1.7%
2006	19.0%
2007	8.9%
2008	-31.9%
2009	22.7%
2010	14.1%
2011	8.4%
2012	10.2%
2013	29.7%

The average annual DJIA return from 1987 to 2013: 11.1%

account cut almost in half by the devastating declines. But let's, for the sake of argument, assume that an investor "gave up" and sold out on November 19, 2008, a day on which the Dow experienced a drop of more than 5 percent (and which happened to mark the bottom in the stock market decline). Using the DJIA as a proxy for her account by selling out on that day the investor locked in her year-to-date loss of 38.2 percent. That means for every dollar she had invested on January 1, 2008, she had only 61.8 cents remaining in her account. But her, perhaps, panicked selling caused even more damage to her investment account. From November 20 through the end of 2008, the Dow returned 10.1 percent for a final, yearly loss of 31.9 percent, which was significant but certainly less than the 38.2 percent realized when our investor sold out on November

19. But let's assume she read this book and realized her mistake and got back into the market on January 1, 2009. She would have gained 22.7 percent over the subsequent 12 months and now would have 75.8 cents of each dollar she invested on January 1, 2008. A loss but a substantially smaller one than if she had not returned to the market. Now suppose her best friend had already read this book and never sold her stock holdings on November 19, 2008. She remained in the market the entire time and by the end of 2009 she had recouped a good portion of her losses and now had 83.5 cents for every dollar invested on January 1, 2008, significantly more than her friend. (To lend some perspective, on a $1 million initial investment selling out on November 19 was an expensive mistake, costing the portfolio $77,000.) We should also note that since the end of 2009 that 83.5 cents (of each dollar invested by our friend who remained in the market) grew to $1.47 through the end of 2013. Significantly better than the first woman who bailed out at the market bottom with 61.8 on every dollar she invested.

Chasing stocks up or down is a flawed strategy that can cost real money. Money you've worked hard to acquire. Stay the course, your course. That is how we grow our wealth.

STICK WITH YOUR DISCIPLINE—REMEMBER THAT WALL STREET IS TERRIBLE AT TURNING POINTS

Maintaining discipline is no doubt tough for all of us. But not as difficult, I think, as it is for Wall Street. During the early 1990s value stock investors were struggling to provide protection in a declining market. Where they would normally do better than the indices, value stocks were performing just as poorly. Or worse. In hindsight, almost precisely when value stocks were poised to produce years of outperformance, one of the major business news magazines published a cover story declaring the end to value investing. The big capitulation. The last pile-on. And that is how a market bottom is achieved, when almost everyone has given up and there is no one left to disappoint. When there are no bulls to be found and we are told over and over again why things are different this time. It is then we would be wise to remember what General George S. Patton, Jr. said: "If everybody is thinking alike, then somebody isn't thinking." And the way to make money in the market is not by thinking like everyone else. We make money by thinking like long-term investors.

Wall Street analysts are not all that different from a middle-school clique. No one wants to stick out unless it is to tout the latest fashion, but most certainly not to decry it. Traveling in a herd, in the same direction, seems to satisfy the dispositions and egos of many experts but it doesn't help their clients make money. If you had the time (and I know you don't—at least not for this assignment) you could watch the way trends are established in the financial media. There really are talking points and they really do move through the public discourse like a human wave at a play-off game. Smooth and relentless. You will hear the pundits (who watch only the pundits) repeat the most popular and palatable theory. As though from their lips to God's ear, as the saying goes. But the herd mentality can only carry a market or stock so far and then beware when the herd turns tail. Because then it is too late to get out.

Take our example of Apple stock in the fall of 2012 when the stock price hit a historical high of just over $700 per share. In chapter 8 we discussed the poor analyst who raised his own price target on Apple when the price powered through his previous price target only to watch it—the very next day—begin an eight-month, approximately 45 percent plunge, where it languished—range bound for months. During that week when Apple stock made its high, 87 percent of Wall Street analysts had a "buy" on the stock. Only 10 percent listed a recommendation of less than "buy." But even more interesting, Apple was among the top fifteen rated stocks in the S&P 500, which placed it in the top 3 percent in terms of positive rankings by Wall Street analysts.

Remember: "If everybody is thinking alike, then someone isn't thinking." I wished I'd said that.

Don't Touch a Hot Stove But Don't Get Scared Out of Stocks Either

I was that kid. The one who touched the hot stove despite the warnings and I still carry the scar today to prove it. Of course, I gave birth to one of those kids, too, but in her case it was a hot curling iron. And, yes, she also carries the scar. But neither of us has chosen the drastic decision to swear off the kitchen or curling our hair. We still engage in those activities but when we do, we take precautions. Appropriate, injury-avoiding precautions.

You *will* get burned in the market. Sooner or later despite your best research efforts and despite following your proven discipline you will lose money on a particular stock during a particular period of time. Just as you will be disappointed by a friend, or a tried and true product or the directions on Google Maps or a trusted hair stylist. But somehow when the market turns against us our first instinct is to swear it off forever. That's probably because we see it as mystical or like gambling or beyond our understanding. When we lack the confidence many of us avoid the activity. But just as you wouldn't abandon an old friend for a lapse, or a trusted stylist for one bad cut or Google Maps for bad directions—well, you get the idea—neither should you abandon investing during periods of difficulty. Think of investing as a "for better or worse activity" and commit for the long haul. Muriel Siebert once said, "You don't have guarantees in this world. You've got to take chances." She was mostly right. There *are* no guarantees in life or investing but buying the stocks of great companies is not "taking chances"; rather it is informed decision-making that comes with risk. Like getting into your car or onto an airplane or riding your bike around the block or, sometimes, even going to the hair stylist.

Be wise. Be prudent. Be bold. Be wary. Be clever and determined and focused on your end goal. Don't be swayed by the crowd; rather, be loyal to your well-thought-out discipline.

CHAPTER 13

Eleven Intelligent Investing Rules—And One More for Good Measure: Rules for Women to Invest By

Let's recap each of our eleven Intelligent Investing Rules plus one.

Intelligent Investing Rule #1: *Having any investment discipline is better than having no discipline at all; once your investment strategy is established, never deviate. (But, if you do fall off the wagon, don't give up, get right back on and stay the course.)*

I knew a fellow who was remarkable for the consistency with which he made poor decisions. In fact, referring to him I once quipped, "His every decision is perfectly incorrect." Of course, that wasn't entirely true. He was bound to be right once in a blue moon but he certainly was an excellent contrary indicator because he was mostly wrong. However, when we employ a sound investment discipline we put ourselves in a position to be mostly right. And being mostly right makes us money over time.

Intelligent Investing Rule #2: *Don't run with the fast crowd: Establish a discipline that meets your objectives. Never chase total return and never, never, never buy a stock in a company you do not understand or does not meet your risk and investing objectives.*

I ran my share of 10k races when I was younger. I was never what you would call a good runner and definitely not what you would call a fast runner. But I muscled my way through and always managed to jog (not crawl) across the finish line. Early on, I learned to avoid the temptation of starting out too fast. While many launched off the starting line, I forced myself to set a reasonable, even slow pace. My goal was finishing, not racing. Staying away from the 100-yard dash crowd when you are running a marathon is sound advice for investing and for life.

Intelligent Investing Rule #3: *Establish your life goals early and stick to your plan. If you think it's hopeless because you've waited too long, remember: The time to save is always now. It is never too late. And remember, too, the only way to "lose" is to not invest at all.*

When I was a kid, saving meant tucking away your pennies and nickels and dimes. Banks provided cardboard savings books with slots for those coins and I would save the milk money my mother gave me, fill my book with nickels, and then deposit the total in a savings account that paid 5 percent per year. Many decades later, I continue to assess my financial goals, I continue to save, but most important, I continue to invest. It is never too late.

Intelligent Investing Rule #4: *Remain dispassionate but diligent. Almost anyone will be able to tell you what is wrong with a company when its stock is cheap. If we buy high-quality companies we can wait for the management team to solve the problems and restore earnings growth; in the meantime we are getting paid via the dividend for the fundamentals to improve.*

Driving presents the clearest example for me of how to remain dispassionate but diligent. Not the routine to the grocery store kind of driving. I am talking about treacherous winding mountain road kind of driving. It terrifies me. Unfortunately. Because I like to go to the mountains. So I've learned to drive dispassionately, but diligently. My secret is not to look too far ahead. To avoid eye contact with the cliff. Instead, I keep focused on the center (guide) line and by doing so, safely reach my destination, intact.

Intelligent Investing Rule #5: *The stock market is a tug-of-war between fear and greed. Buying from fearful sellers and selling to greedy buyers is optimal. But the savvy woman will require more than just good instincts to do so. Develop your discipline, employ the valuation tools we've discussed, and do your research.*

The times in my life when I have had the greatest success acquiring a good deal have been the times when I was willing to walk away, when I tempered my desire, and suppressed my greed. I can't say I've always mastered avarice but when I have, the results have been excellent. If you can simply "drop the rope" in the tug-of-war between the fearful and the greedy you will make sounder and more successful investment decisions.

Intelligent Investing Rule #6: *Since "diversification is the only rational deployment of our ignorance," we must be sure to buy securities that straddle a broad spectrum of economic sectors, to focus on high-quality companies for the long-term, and compile a compatible list of 20 or so names that behave well together, especially when things get out of hand.*

The principle of diversification came alive for me in an unusual way. For many years my husband and I worked for the same firm in their San Francisco office. One day I was informed the San Francisco team would be moving to New York City in sixty days. Just like that our personal lives were upended and because both of us worked for the same company, our income was held hostage to a capricious decision made 2,500 miles away. We couldn't quit because we both would have been out of work. At that point I realized that diversification applied to more than just our stock portfolio—it also applied to our income security. From that point forward, we diversified our careers and have been much more satisfied with the results.

Intelligent Investing Rule #7: *Use financial websites and news for factual content rather than opinions. Only you can decide which investments fit your portfolio and meet your long-term goals.*

Repeat after me: I will not listen to the stock opinions of friends or anonymous investment experts. Full stop.

Intelligent Investing Rule #8: *Focusing on specific qualitative and valuation factors will allow you to avoid Terminally Cheap stocks. Step back from the Wall Street hype as you determine if a Fallen Angel growth stock is an incredible buy or cheap for a good reason. Use periods of underperformance to find great, long-term investment opportunities and don't let the "market scare you out of them."*

Cleaning out my closet prior to a move I was tempted to give away various items. Some of the clothes were just plain ugly or poorly constructed and needed to be tossed. But there was one suit of exceptional quality that for some reason I hung on to, though the cut of the jacket and the hemline were not quite in sync with current fashion. Recently I noticed it was back in style and I have been wearing it regularly since. Some things are cheap because they are cheap but when we buy good quality we can rest on the expectation that eventually the trend will move back in our direction.

Intelligent Investing Rule #9: *Remember investing is an iterative process—we necessarily make adjustments as new information becomes available. Owning the stocks of industry leaders can provide significant excess return to the patient investor; however, there will be times when you will choose to diversify your risk by owning an ETF.*

Many activities in our lives are iterative. Cleaning, exercise, raising our kids, walking the dogs, putting gas in the car, communicating with those we love, paying the bills, shopping—living. To iterate is to say or do again and again and again. Anything of worth to us is worthy of iteration. Investing is no different. Think, observe, research, save, save some more, accumulate shares of your selected stocks, continue to research, and then accumulate some more.

Intelligent Investing Rule #10: *Stocks to own for a lifetime should be the stocks of great companies that are industry and brand leaders with a track record of sound, ethical management. The survivors, who dominate their industry. Build a portfolio of great companies across economic sectors for your lifetime holdings.*

When we buy clothes or furniture or even our first car we are rarely in a position to buy the very best. Our budget just won't allow for it. But when we are buying the stocks of companies we want to own for a lifetime quality is our foremost concern. Buying great companies at a bargain price—a bonus.

Intelligent Investing Rule #11: *High investment management fees are Enemy #1 for women seeking to accumulate wealth. Remember: fees are the single biggest threat to total return in your portfolio.*

Retailers learned long ago if they priced an item at $10.99 consumers would be lured into thinking of the item as a ten-dollar item rather than as an $11.00 item. Real estate agents employ the same strategy when they list a home. But the price is the price no matter what consumers perceive. And investment management fees are real whether you pay them out of your pocket or they are deducted from your account. The impact of those fees compounded over the long-term are considerable. Pay the lowest possible fees you reasonably can. And be sure you are aware of all your costs. Knowledge is the first defense against overpaying.

One more Intelligent Investing Rule for good measure: *Buy stocks like you buy toilet paper—focus on price and yield.*

I don't have much to say here that I haven't said already. Buying large companies that pay a healthy (but not excessive) dividend makes sense for those of us with long-term goals and full lives.

CHAPTER 14

If You Are Going to Hire a Professional Investment Advisor, Let's Make Sure You Hire the Best: You Really Can Do This on Your Own but for Those of You Who Won't, Consider the Following Guidelines

The first time I sat across the conference room table interviewing financial advisors for my own portfolio I was reminded of an old episode of the *The Bob Newhart Show*. The 1970's sitcom chronicled the life of psychologist Bob Newhart and his wife Emily, a grade school teacher. Bob is mortified when he discovers Emily's IQ is much higher than his own and further dismayed when she is invited to join Mensa (a high IQ society that requires members to score amongst the top 2 percent). Bob reluctantly attends a Mensa meeting as her guest, sporting a name tag that includes his IQ (which is high, though not by Mensa standards). Each Mensa member Bob encounters, upon noting his IQ, makes an effort to speak very slowly and very loudly presumably so the less intelligent Newhart can follow along. Their condescension is intentional and obvious. And surprisingly funny. But thirty-plus years later as a prospective investment management client, on the receiving end of similar treatment, I found it a lot less amusing. And not terribly productive.

The research shows that I am not alone in my experience. The Boston Consulting Group revealed that of all the industries that affect their daily lives, women around the world have identified the financial services industry as the one they are most dissatisfied with on both a service and a product level.[1] This statistic should set the financial industry on fire but there appears to have been little change to their marketing and service strategy for women— particularly when it comes to providing relevant education. The study also concluded that more than half those participating in the study believe their wealth managers could improve their service to women and more than 70 percent believe their financial services provider should tailor their approach. Most startling though, according to *Financial Advisor Magazine*, over 70 percent of married women fire their investment advisor within one year of their spouse's death.[2] Since women tend to outlive our husbands on average by at least a decade, hiring a family investment advisor is a decision we should participate in and be satisfied with. (My husband and I ultimately hired a firm and when our results after fees came in subpar, I returned to managing our portfolio and have never looked back.)

Though I am entirely confident each of you can invest successfully for your own portfolio, I realize that for various reasons many of you will choose to work with an advisor. You will be a much a better client for having educated yourself on the investing process. But you will be a more successful client if you are careful to hold your investment advisor accountable to the principles we have learned. Following are five criteria to review prior to hiring your investment advisor.

Make sure your investment advisor can articulate her investment discipline and explain if she would ever diverge from her discipline and, why. When your potential advisor describes her investment discipline you should be able to understand exactly how she intends to go about managing your money. You should be able to re-explain the process to a friend or to your children for that matter—you should understand it that well. No mystique, no opaque descriptions, the process should be so clear that if you wanted to you could follow the same approach yourself. And on the question of divergence from the discipline? The answer should be: never.

In the late 1980s my partners and I started our own investment management firm. Our clients knew our investment discipline almost as well as we did. Not only did we explain it to them in detail before they hired us but we reminded them at each quarterly review meeting how the process was implemented in managing their assets. Most importantly, we promised never to deviate from our discipline. When the financial sector stocks got hit in the early 1990s many of our competitors abandoned their disciplines and sold the stocks, often at their price troughs. They got nervous. They zigged when they should have zagged. They lost their nerve at just the wrong moment and their clients rode the decline and then locked in their losses at the bottom. The sentiment toward financial stocks had become so toxic it took an incredible amount of courage to stick with our discipline and continue to buy the high-quality financial stocks. Two years later our returns were among the top in the country for our style of investing and two of the managers who most notably abandoned their investing discipline were out of business. If your prospective advisor indicates a willingness to compromise her investing discipline you have no assurance she will do so at the right time. In fact, based on the behavioral finance principles we have learned you can be certain the advisor will be more likely to adjust her strategy just when she shouldn't. Recency effect can unduly influence investors in the wrong direction. We also know that because of reversion to the mean our odds of generating strong performance increases if we continue to follow our discipline and allow the market to eventually return to us and its mean performance.

Ask your advisor if all his accounts under management follow the same strategy and hold the same stocks. If not, why not? Also ask to review a sample portfolio of stocks held in like accounts. Your prospective advisor should readily provide you with a copy of the holdings of a representative portfolio during your interview meeting. Scan the holdings and be prepared to ask questions about individual stocks. Questions such as "why do you own this stock?" should be greeted with a ready answer that is accessible and understandable. By the end of the meeting you should have a clear understanding of why the investment manager owns the stocks he owns. You should also understand what it will take for him to sell a stock. But most important you want to know whether or not your assets are being given the same attention as his larger accounts. Will he own the same stocks in your portfolio or does he discriminate among his portfolios based on size and importance?

I once interviewed a manager who seemed entirely unable to describe his discipline. In an effort to ease the process along I asked if I could see a representative portfolio he managed so I could ask stock-specific rather than general questions, hoping this might help him articulate his process more clearly. (Do you find your-self exhibiting this same behavior? Always trying to make others feel comfortable when they should be making you feel comfort-able? Don't! Especially not when you're interviewing a prospec-tive money manager—the very person who should be safekeeping and growing your assets, who should be worried about making his process clear to you rather than you struggling to understand him. The less accommodating you are, the more professional and credible you appear and that will improve your experience on every level.) My alarms went off when he said he didn't really have a representative portfolio. He eventually produced a list of stocks he held across a variety of different accounts. I reviewed the list and asked specific questions like: "If I gave you my assets to manage tomorrow would you buy XYZ stock?" He hemmed and hawed, ultimately admitting he had never really thought about it. I was shocked. Did it show I wondered? I pressed. "OK," I said, "which stocks would you invest in tomorrow if I gave you my money?" He ticked off a few stocks but not the entire list he provided. I singled out another stock. "Would you buy that one?," I asked. "You know, we don't know what to do with that stock—it's too cheap to sell, but I don't really want to buy any more," he replied. The meeting was over. The manager had no articulable discipline and I simply could not entrust my family's assets to him.

Your manager should be able to clearly explain why he owns every stock, whether he would buy those stocks in your portfolio, and provide an explanation as to why or why not. In my experience you will obtain much better and more consistent performance if your advisor treats all of his accounts the same. You will be priori-tized just like his other accounts and more likely to receive returns representative of the historical returns he has achieved. Consistency and full disclosure are paramount when selecting an investment advisor.

Now that you understand the advisor's process, make sure her style and risk parameters match your financial goals. Of course you don't want to hire a risk-averse manager if you are interested in taking higher levels of risk. Similarly you don't want to hire a growth manager if you have a value bias, no matter how well she explains her process. The advisor's characteristics are easy to confirm, though you may have to ask her to translate the meaning of the risk and return statistics from investment management-ese to English. All of that information should be readily available to you. In addition to risk and return characteristics, make sure to ask about portfolio turnover. This will help you assess what your tax liability may be if the monies are in a taxable account. High turnover means that your tax bill will be potentially large and most certainly your costs (to execute the transactions) will be high. Since transaction costs are deducted from the total return you receive, these costs are real. Additionally, high turnover managers tend to take more risk. If a manager claims to be a low risk manager but reports a high turnover rate you know something isn't quite right and you may want to continue looking. But if the portfolio manager's turnover matches the risk parameter you are seeking remember to consider the implications for your tax bill. We have already discussed the rates associated with short-term versus long-term gains; short-term gains are paid at your income tax rate while long-term gains can be much lower (again depending on your income tax bracket) so that information is also important to secure from the potential advisor. What percentage of her gains are long-term, what percentage are short-term? And will she be willing to engage in tax loss harvesting at the end of the year to offset gains? If she is not willing to do so and you are still interested in having a professional manager for your assets you may want to consider a mutual fund. You will likely save money on the fee for effectively the same level of service. When I was a professional money manager we routinely worked with our clients and their advisors at year-end to maximize their tax situation. It is, after all, the client's money—your money—and your advisor should be as interested in growing and preserving your wealth as you are. Though taxes sometimes get overlooked by investors—after all if you are paying taxes that means that you are making money—consider that a 10 percent return quickly becomes an 8.5 percent return assuming (best case) all of the manager's gains are long-term. Taxes and high fees will erode your wealth accumulation faster than just about anything else.

Now that you understand the advisor's process, have confirmed that her process meets your risk and return parameters, make sure her track record is outstanding as well. The manager's performance track record should be available to you. There are specific industry rules outlining how performance is to be calculated and reported. Importantly the rules require that all accounts are included in the calculation to prevent the manager from cherry-picking only the best-performing accounts and reporting those results to prospective clients (another argument for a manager who manages all accounts exactly the same). Reviewing her performance will allow you to compare her results to that of the market, and often a peer group of comparable managers. You will also be able to analyze the manager's volatility of total return from year to year. And, one of the most revealing criteria requires that investment managers report their performance net of (or after) fees paid. These performance rules provide a useful tool for determining how well an advisor has performed for her clients based on the fee paid and the risk taken all the while comparing her to her peers.

You may not be hiring your manager simply based on her previous performance but it is an important way to measure the effectiveness of her investment discipline and her ability to implement it. Investment performance is an investment manager's report card. At the end of the day, performance is the product you receive for the fee you pay. All things being equal you want your advisor to be an "A" student.

Ask your potential advisor about his firm's compensation structure. You are entitled to know this no matter how uncomfortable it makes you feel to ask. So, ask! Understanding how well your potential manager is paid will help you better determine whether he is likely to remain at the firm and remain focused on the management of your account. For better or worse, the investment management industry is a highly compensated one. If your manager is good you want to make sure he is being compensated at or above the industry compensation level. Otherwise he is a ripe target for a competitor. And then you are back to square one, stuck looking for a new manager for your assets.

As a professional money manager we were asked this question routinely. I cannot recall a time when we were not hired because a potential client felt that we made too much money, but I can recall a large potential client choosing not to hire us because our compensation was below the industry median and he was worried we would leave and go somewhere else. And eventually he was right—we did. We left the large bank we worked for to start our own firm and we made sure that our compensation structure was above the industry median from day one. Firms that provide a fair compensation structure and collegial work environment will keep their professionals and that will enhance your portfolio performance.

Make sure you like and feel comfortable with your advisor. Trust is more important than competence. Just ask Bernie Madoff's clients. If you don't like your advisor and trust your advisor you will not enjoy a successful relationship. Women repeatedly report that while the gender of their investment advisor is irrelevant, they desire proactive and clear communication. They seek personalized attention but that doesn't translate to lunches or meaningless phone calls. Women are busy, extremely busy, and we want to receive information in a clear, concise form and in a way that is convenient for us. If not, like the women cited in the study at the beginning of the chapter, we are likely to be dissatisfied with our financial partner—one of the most important professional relationships we will establish.

Your assets must be protected; they most likely will be one of the primary gifts you leave your heirs. Given how hard you work to save and invest for your future family financial goals, ensuring the growth and protection of your assets is, therefore, one of the most important decisions you can make. We often spend a great deal of time determining which car to buy. We read the reviews and the safety ratings, we test drive, we talk to people who own the same car, and we test drive again. We grill the salesman on features and financing terms; we negotiate the price and negotiate some more. Until finally, we settle on the best possible car at the best possible price. We should expend the same effort and discernment when hiring a financial services provider because the long-term ramifications are much more critical to our future.

I once had the privilege to manage a large portfolio for the US Army. At each quarterly meeting the colonel in charge of the Army's funds thanked me for my "satisfactory" performance. For years his comments bothered me. I didn't strive to be satisfactory, though by his reckoning "satisfactory" was apparently a very good thing. Still, I continued to work hard to deliver exceptional returns and one day he acknowledged our performance in a comment I remember to this day—"Nancy," he told me, "last quarter was better than satisfactory." Knowing he was watching very closely, that he had extraordinarily high standards regarding the assets he was responsible for safeguarding for the Army kept his face ever before me as I carried out my management duties. The colonel became a symbol of all of my clients—the face if you will—each morning when the market opened and each afternoon at the close. His objective, his mission, was my mission, which is exactly as it should be.

It is, after all, your money. And your future.

Appendix: Investment Websites

- **Bespoke Investment Group:** http://www.bespokeinvest. com/thinkbig
- **Bloomberg:** www.bloomberg.com
- **Charles Schwab:** https://www.schwab.com
- **CNBC.com:** http://www.cnbc.com
- **Dividend.com:** http://www.dividend.com
- **Dividends and Income Daily:** http://www.dividendsandin-comedaily.com/
- **Dividend Channel:** http://www.dividendchannel.com/
- **Fidelity:** https://www.fidelity.com/
- **GuruFocus:** http://www.gurufocus.com
- **Investopedia:** http://www.investopedia.com/
- **MarketWatch:** http://www.marketwatch.com
- **McGraw Hill Financial:** http://us.spindices.com
- **The Motley Fool:** http://www.fool.com/
- **Seeking Alpha:** http://seekingalpha.com/
- **S&P Dow Jones Indices:** http://us.spindices.com/
- **Stock Rover:** http://www.stockrover.com/
- **Yahoo! Finance:** http://finance.yahoo.com/
- **YCharts:** http://ycharts.com/
- **Vanguard:** https://investor.vanguard.com/home/

GLOSSARY OF INVESTMENT TERMS: MASTERING THE LANGUAGE WILL PROVIDE YOU WITH CONFIDENCE AND WILL BROADEN YOUR KNOWLEDGE BASE

I suppose one of the most off-putting things for most new investors is understanding the jargon. Whether it serves as a form of clarification or segregation, language can alienate and overwhelm new investors. But as is often the case, the special language, the acronyms, the catch phrases are simply one way of saying something else. For example, take the word equity. Most of us understand equity in terms of our home. If the value of our home today is more than we owe we understand the difference to be our equity. But investors also refer to shares of stocks as equities. And in this case the term represents an ownership interest. So the terms stock or equity convey the same meaning and are often used interchangeably and both mean ownership. That is not so different from the term equity when applied to your home. The difference between the home's value and what you owe is your true ownership; a share of a stock—an equity interest—represents your ownership in a company. In short, with modest effort, investing terms are accessible.

Our objective is not to master every investing idiom but to develop a keen understanding of foundational investment principles. We want to control the variables we can control and the foremost is knowledge. Knowing what we are buying and why we are buying it reduces our risk and the sense that investing is gambling. Investing is akin to building equity—to buying a portion of a corporation and waiting for it to appreciate. Building equity in our homes is desirable but buying equity in really great companies is how we generate wealth.

- **Active management:** Investors who practice active management assume that the stock market is not efficient and through superior research and stock selection they can identify mispriced stocks and in doing so perform better than the overall market (often measured by the major stock market indices: the Dow Jones Industrial Average, the S&P 500, or the NASDAQ).
- **Annual report or 10-k:** All publicly traded companies are required by the Securities and Exchange Commission (SEC) to file a 10-k or annual report providing a comprehensive overview of the firm's business activities. The annual report is studied by securities analysts and investors to better understand the firm's financial condition and earnings growth expectations.
- **Asset allocation:** Any investment plan employs an allocation to stocks and bonds or cash equivalents among other things. Depending on our investment time horizon and ultimate goal, our willingness to trade-off potential volatility for investment return will influence how our assets are allocated.
- **Bear market:** A bear market is defined as a sustained decline of 20 percent or more as measured by the stock market indices. The period usually extends over a period of multiple months or even years. A one-day decline—like Black Monday's precipitous fall of over 20 percent—would be characterized as a correction versus a bear market because of its short duration.
- **Behavioral economics:** Behavioral economics challenge the basic assumption that forms the foundation of economics: that individuals act rationally when making financial decisions. Behavioral economics studies our biases, emotions, and faulty assumptions—the psychology—that influence financial decisions made under uncertainty. (The condition, one might argue, under which every financial decision is ultimately made.) Understanding the underlying theories of behavioral economics can enhance our understanding of our investing selves.
- **Blue-chip stocks:** The blue-chip is a large-cap, industry leader with the kind of brand dominance that makes it a household name. The kind of stocks we want to consider to own for a lifetime. Dividends are usually (though not always) paid by blue-chip companies.

- **Bull market:** A bull market then is a market where stocks are rising, a market characterized by optimism. It is possible to experience declines in a bull market period (in fact, many investors are pleased by a small correction to let the market settle and regroup) but the extended trend is positive.
- **Buy-side analyst:** A buy-side analyst works for an investment management firm that manages the assets of clients via separate accounts, mutual funds, or ETFs. The term refers to the fact that investment management firms tend to "buy" research from Wall Street or **"sell-side"** firms. Buy-side analysts are typically assigned to broad industry groups or entire sectors and are charged with the task of supporting the firm's portfolio managers in selecting stocks for their client portfolios.
- **Capital appreciation and total return:** Capital appreciation is the growth, or appreciation, of your investment in excess of the price you paid for that investment. Capital equals money so capital appreciation measures the growth of the money you invested. Separate from capital appreciation is the **dividend return**. It is similar to the interest you receive from your bank but, and this is a big but, dividend payments often grow as the company's earnings grow. **Total return** includes capital appreciation, the compounding of dividend payments, and the growth in those dividend payments.
- **Correlation:** In financial terms, correlation measures how two investments move together. The measurement ranges from -1 to +1 (the correlation coefficient). If two securities are perfectly correlated (think: rise and fall at the same time or in lock-step) their correlation coefficient equals +1. If two securities are, conversely, perfectly negatively correlated (coefficient of -1) one security will rise while the other falls. If two securities are determined to have zero correlation we expect that they will act entirely independent of each other, with no expected similarity of pattern.
- **Defined-benefit plan:** A defined-benefit plan is a retirement plan (or pension) sponsored by the company. The benefits to the employee are calculated according to length of service and salary and provide a guaranteed monthly payout at the time of

retirement. Of course, each plan carries different restrictions unique to each company but the primary, defining characteristic of a defined-benefit plan is that the company takes on the responsibility of funding and managing retirement assets for their employees. These plans are primarily offered by government agencies and are rarely offered in the private sector any longer.

- **Defined-contribution plan:** Defined-contribution plans are most typically characterized by the 401(k). In these plans the employee contributes directly to her company-sponsored plan and is responsible for selecting from a company-designed and managed menu of investment products. While many corporations match some portion of the employee's contribution most of the responsibility for the savings rate and investment selection falls on the individual.

- **Dividend:** Not all companies pay a dividend but those that do determine the amount of the dividend based on a portion of earnings. The dividend is set by the board of directors (which often includes company management) and is quoted to shareholders as a dollar amount per share per year. In my experience larger companies tend to have a "dividend paying culture," one that endeavors to pay investors (via the dividend) a portion of long-term sustainable earnings power. At these companies dividends grow in line with earnings, which results in not only a reliable, but also a growing income stream.

- **Dividend payout ratio:** The payout ratio is calculated by dividing the company's dividend per share by the earnings per share. The payout ratio is important because it tells investors how much of the company's earnings are being committed to the dividend. Determining the payout ratio helps investors determine if the dividend is safe.

- **Dividend yield:** The dividend yield of a stock is calculated by dividing the annual dividend per share by the price of the stock per share. For example, if a stock pays an annual dividend per share of $1 and the price of the stock is $40 then the dividend yield is 2.5 percent. 1/40 = 2.5 percent. Obviously as the price of the stock moves up or down the dividend yield will change accordingly. Similarly if the dividend is increased or decreased the dividend yield will adjust.

- **Dollar-cost averaging:** Our most relevant real-life experience in dollar-cost averaging is our 401(k) account. Each month we invest a pre-specified amount into our 401(k) plan investments. By scheduling our investment into the market, no matter current levels, we dollar-cost average our investment.

- **Dow Jones Industrial Average (DJIA or DOW):** Charles H. Dow developed the Dow Jones Industrial Average index in the late 1800s. He unveiled his twelve-stock industrial index in the spring of 1896; in 1916 the average was expanded to twenty stocks and in 1928 to thirty stocks. The average has remained at thirty stocks, though the underlying companies have changed over the years to remain representative of the overall US economy. The index is price-weighted, which means that the stocks with the highest price influence the performance of the index more. (Recall that price does not necessarily mean a stock is expensive. For example: Apple with a share price of approximately $550 is trading at around 11x earnings and is actually inexpensive compared to Facebook at approximately $55, which is trading at 52x earnings. Despite its higher per share price, Apple is less "expensive" than Facebook but would have a much larger influence on the performance of the Dow Jones.)

- **Earnings estimates:** Estimating future earnings is one of the most important jobs of a **sell-side analyst**. These analysts employ guidance from company management, develop forecasting models, and conduct primary research to determine sales and earnings growth trends. These estimates form the most important input for valuing the company's stock price using the forward **price-to-earnings ratio** (p/e). The p/e depends largely on analyst earnings estimates, which in turn aids the analyst in establishing a price target for the stock.

- **Economic sector:** Economic sectors are comprised of industries. There are ten economic sectors (some breakdowns include only eight depending on the criteria employed): consumer discretionary, consumer staples, energy, financials, health care, industrials, information technology, materials, telecommunications services, and utilities. Arguably some companies' businesses straddle sectors like Johnson & Johnson, with a broad reach into pharmaceuticals as well as consumer staples. A diversified portfolio will include exposure across all or most sectors because companies within the same industries tend to be relatively positively correlated (and will often rise and fall together); therefore, investors should own stocks in all or most sectors to smooth out portfolio performance.

- **Exchange-traded funds (ETFs):** An ETF is actually a security that tracks an index (sector, geography, commodity, etc.) and trades like a stock. The primary differentiation between an ETF and a mutual fund is that an ETF can be traded throughout the day since it is priced like a stock, in real time, and a mutual fund is only priced at the end of the day when the net asset value or NAV is calculated. ETFs, therefore, are more liquid and flexible investments when compared to mutual funds.
- **Fallen Angel growth stocks:** A Fallen Angel growth stock is a former growth stock that has fallen from favor. The question facing investors is whether the fall is a temporary stumble or a permanent transition for the company from growth to value. Fallen Angels are sometimes also referred to as growth stocks trading at a reasonable price and can provide investors with exceptional returns if and when the company management returns the stock to growth stock status.
- **Fixed income security (bond):** A fixed income security or bond is one that guarantees a fixed payment of income over a pre-specified period of time. At the end of the duration of the term the original investment is returned. If an investor buys a $1,000 ten-year government bond at 3 percent, she will earn $30 per year on her $1,000 investment for ten years and then receive repayment of her $1,000 at the end of the term. Because the return is guaranteed it is lower than that potentially earned investing in riskier securities like stocks.
- **Futures:** Futures contracts can be obtained on just about any liquid investment available and are an agreement to buy or sell a set amount of a financial instrument (a stock or stock index, for

example) or a commodity. Buying and selling futures contracts involves a higher level of risk and I am not advocating purchase of future contracts, well, ever. But I do watch the index futures traded each morning to inform me how the market is trading prior to the open each day.

- **Growth assets:** The term growth assets typically refers to stocks. The value of your capital investment may fluctuate but over time is expected to grow at a pace in excess of inflation.

- **Growth stocks:** Growth stocks are those whose earnings are expected to grow faster than the average growth in the stocks that comprise the overall market averages. Growth stocks tend not to pay a dividend since investors expect management to invest excess profits in future growth initiatives such as research and development or acquisitions, for example. Historically, some investors have referred to growth stocks as glamor stocks because of the cachet associated with owning some high-profile growth stocks.

- **Growth at a reasonable price (GARP):** GARP investing seeks to purchase stocks with above-market earnings growth opportunities that are trading at or below-market valuations. Our Fallen Angel growth stocks fall into the GARP category, though not all GARP stocks are Fallen Angels. One of the objectives of GARP investing is said to be the avoidance of either extreme of growth or value investing but from a practical standpoint it simply makes good sense to buy the fastest growing companies you can at the cheapest valuation.

- **Hedge fund:** A hedge fund is usually offered via a private partnership to investors who meet certain net-worth requirements. The funds tend to require large initial investments and are relatively illiquid—usually requiring advanced notice if a withdrawal is required. Unlike mutual funds, hedge funds for the most part are unregulated since they serve sophisticated investors who presumably do not require the protection of regulators. The funds employ riskier and varied strategies than the typical mutual fund, often using leverage and taking **short** as well as **long positions** in stocks. Hedge funds also charge much higher fees.

- **Heuristic:** Heuristic is from the Greek: to discover. We use the term today to mean problem solving via trial-and-error methods.
- **Index fund:** An index fund is a mutual fund that tracks a specific index like the S&P 500, seeking only to perform in line with the index. The advantage of index funds is that they carry much lower fees than those of actively managed funds and over time tend to perform as well as or better than many mutual funds. ETFs also track indices (including the S&P 500) but the term typically refers to mutual funds.
- **Initial public offering (IPO):** An IPO is the first sale of stock by a company to the public. IPOs are underwritten by investment banking firms (like Goldman, JPMorgan Chase, and others) to determine the price of the offering, timing, and number of shares to be offered. Often, these shares are offered to big clients of the investment banking firm and are difficult for individual investors to acquire. They are also, for the most part, risky investments.
- **Investment strategy:** We have identified three investment strategies for stock investing. There are certainly more but our focus is on growth, value, and growth at a reasonable price (a variation on both the value and growth strategies). These strategies can be employed in any size category of company. Size is measured by **market capitalization** (see below).
- **Long position:** A long position, for our purposes, is simply when an investor owns shares of a company's stock. If I own shares in Tiffany & Co., I am long Tiffany.
- **Market capitalization or market cap:** The market capitalization of a company is simply the value of all the shares outstanding (held by investors) multiplied by the current stock price. This measure tells investors how big the company is in a way that is more measurable against other companies than sales or earnings. Investors segment stocks into capitalization groups such as micro, small, mid, and large capitalization for purposes of allocating investing dollars.
- **Momentum:** Momentum investors watch the rate of acceleration of a stock's price movement (either up or down). The belief

is that the stock price is more likely to continue moving in the same direction rather than change directions (though we might argue this point) and so they make buy and sell decisions based on that expectation. Momentum investors almost always invest in growth stocks that tend to demonstrate the most dramatic price movements.

- **Multiple expansion:** Multiple expansion refers to the increase in the p/e ratio or, as it is sometimes called, p/e multiple. As investor confidence increases or earnings accelerate, investors are often willing to pay more for future earnings growth, thereby increasing the p/e. The p/e, remember, has two variables: price and earnings. The p/e will increase if either one or both variables increase. Consequently, multiple expansion should be analyzed as to whether the price alone is expanding (which might argue that the stock/market is overvalued) or if earnings are expanding as well. Multiple expansion is neither good or bad without understanding the underlying earnings fundamentals for an individual stock or the market as a whole.

- **Mutual fund:** A mutual fund pools the money of many investors for the purpose of investing that money for capital gains. Mutual funds provide small, individual investors with the opportunity to obtain the services of professional money managers, often available only to those investors with large sums of money. Because the assets are pooled, the fund calculates a net asset value at the close of the market each day. This sets a price for investors buying or selling the fund and is the means by which performance is calculated for the fund and, therefore, for the participants in the fund. Mutual funds are regulated and are required to produce a prospectus for investors, which serves a similar purpose as the 10-k and proxy statement offered to investors by individual companies.

- **NASDAQ/The National Association of Securities Dealers:** The NASDAQ is an electronic market of 5,000 stocks. Unlike the **New York Stock Exchange** (NYSE) that uses designated market makers or specialists assigned to each stock and who are charged with maintaining an "orderly market" in the trading of a specific security, the NASDAQ is an automated and centralized quotation and trading system.

- **New York Stock Exchange (NYSE):** Often referred to as the Big Board, the NYSE is the largest stock exchange in the world as measured by market capitalization. The value of the companies trading on the Big Board was over $16 trillion in 2013. Average daily trading volume was approximately $169 billion in 2013.

- **Opportunity cost:** The opportunity cost is represented by the difference between the appreciation of an investment made compared to the return you could earn in an investment not made. Purchasing the Donna Karan cashmere sweater discussed in chapter 1 cost me $1,099, but my opportunity cost was $11,430 in lost appreciation had I, instead, invested the $1,099 in IBM (the alternative transaction discussed in chapter 1).

- **Portfolio turnover:** Portfolio turnover measures how quickly the assets in a particular account are "turned over" or bought and sold by the fund or account manager. The measurement period is one year. Turnover is important to investors because trading costs are subtracted from the total return they receive and because long-term and short-term stock gains come with a corresponding tax bill. Consequently, if a manager generates a 10 percent total return with 25 percent turnover and another manager generates a 10 percent total return with 100 percent turnover, the after-tax return to the client/investor is likely to be much higher with the first manager who achieved the same total return with fewer taxable transactions.

- **Price-to-earnings ratio (p/e):** The p/e is a ratio that measures the price investors are willing to pay per share of stock for the corresponding earnings per share produced by the company. This ratio is also calculated for a collection of stocks like those represented in the stock indices like the S&P 500. Often investors compare the p/e of a particular stock against the p/e of the S&P 500 to determine a stock's relative attractiveness. Because the p/e is a ratio, changes in the underlying variables—price and earnings—will obviously cause the p/e to rise or fall. The p/e is one of the most widely quoted stock statistics and is calculated on a trailing and twelve-month estimated basis.

- **Price-to-sales ratio (p/s):** The p/s ratio or PSR measures the price investors are paying for a company's trailing sales. This is an important measure when a company's earnings may be depressed because of special items or reinvestment in growth. Most common as a valuation measure for growth stocks (those companies who are reinvesting earnings in future growth) the p/s ratio can also be helpful in valuing Fallen Angel growth stocks whose earnings have suffered a short-term decline.

- **Protection assets:** Protection assets are usually bonds or cash. These vehicles protect the capital invested. In the case of cash, the capital is liquid and does not fluctuate in value. In the case of bonds, the value of the bond may fluctuate somewhat during the term of investment but the entire capital investment is returned to the investor at the end of the prespecified term. While protection assets may preserve capital they do not ensure that the investor is compensated for the erosion of inflation on the value of her underlying capital investment.

- **Proxy statement:** All publicly traded companies are required by the SEC to provide investors with a proxy statement, with information on shareholder initiatives, election of the board of directors, and proposals for senior executive compensation (among other things) that will be voted on at the company's annual meeting. Shareholders do not need to attend the annual meeting to cast a vote; they can vote their proxy by mail. The proxy statement is the "voter's guide" to the issues and directors under consideration at the company's annual meeting.

- **Reversion to the mean:** Reversion to the mean or regression to the mean as it is also known argues: the greater the deviation from the mean, the greater the probability that the next measured event will deviate from the mean far less. The mean stock market return, for example, is approximately 9 percent for the last 100 years so we could extrapolate: extreme stock outperformance relative to the mean (9 percent in our example) is more likely to be followed by a less extreme performance (say 1 percent).

- **Recency effect:** Recency effect is the tendency of individuals to remember a more recent experience better than a previous experience. For example, when given a long list of words, most people can most easily remember the words at the end of the list. In behavioral economics this is also referred to as "availability." For investors, recency effect can serve to bias investing decisions based on recent market performance. Whether up or down we tend to extrapolate the recent event into the future. If the market is going up investor behavior is more likely to act on expectations of a rising market. The converse is also true. Both tendencies are dangerous.
- **Standard & Poors 500 Index (S&P 500):** The S&P 500 is an index of 500 US companies selected by a team of analysts and economists at Standard and Poors. The companies are selected based on size and industry grouping, among other factors. The stocks in the S&P 500 represent approximately 75 percent of the value of all US stocks traded. In other words, the S&P 500 index serves as a benchmark of the performance of the major US stocks. Over $5 trillion dollars is benchmarked or invested in index funds that track the S&P 500.
- **Sell-side analyst:** Sell-side analysts can work for large investment banks and brokerages or small, independent research firms. What differentiates them from buy-side analysts is their focus on specific industries and responsibility for generating earnings forecasting models and buy and sell recommendations. Sell-side analysts produce reports and earnings models purchased by buy-side firms (hence the names buy and sell-side) that use the data to inform their portfolio decisions for the assets they manage.
- **Share repurchase program:** Share repurchase programs are initiated by the company to buy back shares of their stock from the marketplace. Doing so reduces the number of shares outstanding and consequently increases the earnings per share. Additionally, share buybacks are often perceived by the market as an indication that the management believes the stock is undervalued. However, it can also mean (as it has in recent years) that management has plenty of free cash flow or access to

cash at cheap rates and has not identified a better place (such as acquisitions or earnings growth initiatives) to deploy the cash.

- **Short position:** When an investor takes a short position in a stock he is expecting the stock to decline. The investor borrows shares of the stock from a third party, usually a broker, and sells them in the open market. He is expecting to be able to buy the shares back cheaper at a later date and return them to the original owner, thus securing a large profit. Of course, the investor must pay a fee to borrow the shares and is making, in essence, a bet that the shares will decline by taking a short position. This is not a strategy recommended for readers of The Women's Guide to Successful Investing who are interested in investing for the long-term.

- **Smart money:** This term is used to represent the experienced, "in-the know" Wall Street crowd. Their investment decisions are assumed to be better and more insightful than those of the individual investor. Perhaps it is true, but no empirical research exists (that I have found) to prove it.

- **Stock (equity):** A share of stock represents an ownership or equity stake in a company that has issued stock in an initial public offering (IPO). If you are a stockholder (also referred to as shareholder), you own a proportionate share in the company's assets, which include the company's earnings. You may be paid a share of the company's earnings in the form of dividends, which contribute to a portion of your total return. Share price increases form the remainder of your return.

- **Stock tickers** are established so stocks can be traded by your broker or discount broker on the floor of the New York Stock Exchange (NYSE) or the NASDAQ in a company you desire to own. The unique symbol is selected by the company to facilitate trading of their securities. Think of it is a Twitter handle—an identifier unique to one individual or, in this case, one company. Tickers can be found on any financial or investing website by typing in the company name.

- **Tax lots:** Tax lot accounting is provided by your broker or investment manager. These lots represent each trade completed for each security in your portfolio. The benefit is that you know exactly what you've paid for each share over time and the accounting provides the necessary information when it is time to tax loss harvest.

- **Tax loss harvesting:** Investors who are conscious of the tax implications of selling stocks engage in tax loss harvesting. By reviewing tax lots the investor can take short-term or long-term gains or losses to offset other transactions in their portfolio, thus minimizing taxable gains. Tax loss harvesting is typically executed near the end of the year and requires the investor to wait thirty days before re-purchasing any shares that were sold specifically for tax purposes (but that the investor still may want to own for the long-term).

- **Value stocks:** Value stocks are typically characterized by low p/e's and/or high dividend yields. These stocks are considered to be undervalued based on the price paid for future earnings and future earnings growth. Value stocks tend to exhibit lower volatility than growth stocks and, according to multiple research studies conducted over the years, tend to outperform growth stocks over the long-term.

- **Volatility** measures the variance of the return of a particular stock compared to the stock index. The greater the variance or volatility, the riskier the stock is generally considered to be.

NOTES

PREFACE

1. Lusardi, Annamaria and Mitchell, Olivia S. (2006) "Financial Literacy and Retirement Preparedness: Evidence and Implications for Financial Education." University of Michigan Retirement Research Center, working paper.
2. Bajtelsmit, Vickie L. and Bernasek, Alexandra. (1996) "Why Do Women Invest Differently Than Men?" Financial Counseling and Planning, 7, 1–10.

1 WEALTH ACCUMULATION IS AN ATTITUDE: INVESTING FOR YOUR FUTURE REQUIRES A FEW GOALS AND MUCH LESS CAPITAL THAN YOU THINK

1. Benartzi, Shlomo Benartzi. "Do You Know Why You Aren't Saving Enough for Your Future?" Allianz Global Investors, http://www .allianzusa.com/investments/investing-insights/behavioral -finance/.html.
2. Damisch, Peter, Monish Kumar, Anna Zakrzewski, and Natalia Zhiglinskaya (July 2010) "Leveling the Playing Field, Upgrading the Wealth Management Experience for Women." The Boston Consulting Group, www.bcg.perspectives.com.

2 WHY WOMEN MAKE EXCELLENT INVESTORS: WOMEN INHERENTLY DISPLAY THE TRAITS REQUIRED FOR SUCCESSFUL INVESTING

1. Prudential. (2012–2013) "Financial Experience & Behaviors Among Women."
2. Barber, Brad M. and Odean, Terrance. (February 2001) "Boys Will Be Boys: Gender, Overconfidence, and Common Stock Investment." The Quarterly Journal of Economics, 261–292.
3. Barber, Brad M. and Odean, Terrance. (April 2000) "Trading Is Hazardous to Your Wealth: The Common Stock Investment Performance of Individual Investors." The Journal of Finance, 55(2), 773–806.
4. National Council for Research on Women. (June 2009) "Women in Fund Management." New York, pp. 1–40.
5. Abrams, Dan. (2011) Man Down: Proof Beyond a Reasonable Doubt That Women Are Better Cops, Drivers, Gamblers, Spies, World Leaders, Beer Tasters, Hedge Fund Managers and Just About Everything Else. New York: Abrams Image.

6. Tversky, Amos and Kahneman, Daniel. (September 1974) "Judgment under Uncertainty: Heuristics and Biases." Science, 185, 1124–1131.
7. Epstein, Gene. (May 13, 2013) "We Were Right." Barron's.

3 In Order to Get There We Need to Know Where We Are Going: Establishing Financial Goals Informs Successful Savings and Investment Plans

1. Prudential. (2012–2013) "Financial Experience & Behaviors Among Women." www.prudential.com/women
2. Ruffenach, Glenn. (October 28, 2013) "The So-You-Think-You're-Ready-for-Retirement Quiz." The Wall Street Journal.
3. Benartzi, Shlomo. (2012) "Part 2—Overcoming Investor Paralysis: Invest More Tomorrow." Allianz Global Investors, http://befi.allianzgi.com/en/Publications/Documents/Part%202-%20Investor%20Paralysis.pdf
4. Kahneman, Daniel and Tversky, Amos. (March 1979) "Prospect Theory: An Analysis of Decision Under Risk." Econometrica, 47(2), 263–291.
5. Ibbotson, Roger G. and Kaplan, Paul D. (January/February 2000) "Does Asset Allocation Policy Explain 40, 90, or 100 Percent of Performance?" Financial Analysts Journal, 56(1), 26–33.
6. TIAA-CREF. (July 1998) "Investing for a Distant Goal: Optimal Asset Allocation and Attitudes toward Risk." Research Dialogues Issue Number 56, pp. 1–11.

4 Developing an Investment Discipline That Will Achieve our Goals: For the Diligent Student and Practitioner, Investing—Like Any Skill—Can Be Perfected; Matching Our Investment Strategy with Our Goals Is Paramount

1. Horner, M. S. (1968) "Sex Differences in Achievement Motivation and Performance in Competitive and Noncompetitive Situations." Unpublished doctoral dissertation, University of Michigan.
2. Fama, Eugene F. and French, Kenneth R. (December 1998) "Value versus Growth: The International Evidence." The Journal of Finance, 53(6), 1975–1999.
3. Lakonishok, Josef, Shleifer, Andrei and Vishny, Robert W. (1994) "Contrarian investment, extrapolation, and risk." Journal of Finance, 49, 1541–1578.
4. Haugen, Robert. (1995) The New Finance: The Case against Efficient Markets (Englewood Cliffs, NJ: Prentice Hall).
5. Barad, Michael W. (November 2003) "Ibbotson Style Indices: A Comprehensive Set of Growth and Value Data." A Working White Paper (6th draft).
6. Kapadia, Reshma. (November 2, 2013) "Good Things Come to…" Barron's.
7. Bary, Andrew. (October 19, 2013) "AT&T's High-Yield Attraction." Barron's.
8. Lazo, Shirley A. (October 26, 2013) "Honeywell Revs Up Dividend." Barron's.
9. Arnott, Robert D. (March–April 2003) "Dividends and the Three Dwarfs." Financial Analysts Journal, 59(2), 4–6.
10. Schwert, William G. (1990) "Indexes of U.S. Stock Prices from 1802 to 1987." Journal of Business, 63(3), 399–442.

11. Heartland Funds. (2012) "Dividends: A Review of Historical Returns." www.heartlandfunds.com

5   DEVELOPING AN INVESTMENT DISCIPLINE THAT WILL ACHIEVE OUR
GOALS—CONTINUED: THE STOCK MARKET IS A TUG-OF-WAR BETWEEN
FEAR AND GREED; ARM YOURSELF WITH THE TOOLS TO SUCCEED

1. De Long, J. Bradford, et al. (1990) "Noise Trader Risk in Financial Markets." University of Chicago Press.
2. Sharpe, William F. (March–April 2013) "The Arithmetic of Investment Expenses." Financial Analysts Journal, 69(2), 34–41.
3. Ellis, Charles D., CFA. (May–June 2012) "Investment Management Fees Are (Much) Higher Than You Think." Financial Analysts Journal, 68(3), 4–6.
4. Kinnel, Russel. (August 2010) "How Expense Ratios and Star Ratings Predict Success." Morningstar FundInvestor, 18(12), 1–5.

6   CONSTRUCT YOUR PORTFOLIO LIKE A DINNER PARTY INVITATION LIST:
HOLDINGS SHOULD BE BALANCED AND BEHAVE WELL IF
THINGS GET OUT OF HAND

1. Brinson, Gary P., et al. (January–February 1995) "Determinants of Portfolio Performance." Financial Analysts Journal, 133–138.
2. Hotz, Robert Lee. (December 10, 2013) "Brain Wiring in Men Versus Women." The Wall Street Journal.

9   A CASE STUDY OF A STALLED LUXURY BRAND—COACH, INC.:
WHETHER COACH BAGS FIT YOUR BUDGET OR STYLE, WE CAN
LEARN A GREAT DEAL FROM THIS FORMER DARLING

1. Williams, Christopher C. (December 7, 2013) "Coach's New Bag of Tricks." Barron's.

10   STOCKS TO OWN FOR A LIFETIME: IDENTIFYING INDUSTRY
LEADERS PROVIDES THE CONVICTION REQUIRED TO BUY STOCKS
WE ARE WILLING TO HOLD FOR DECADES

1. Dillard, Annie. (1989) The Writing Life (New York: HarperCollins).
2. Bary, Andrew. (December 28, 2013) "A Lion in Winter." Barron's.
3. Hough, Jack. (June 2013) "Six Stocks That Could Double in Five Years," Barron's.
4. Evans, Bob. (October 9, 2012) "Larry Ellison Doesn't Get the Cloud: The Dumbest Idea of 2013." Forbes.
5. Rehak, Judith. (March 23, 2002) "Tylenol Made a Hero of Johnson & Johnson: The Recall that Started Them All." The New York Times.
6. Goodman, Beverly. (January 6, 2014) "Back To School: Fama, French Discuss Their Work." Barron's.

11   ETFs TO OWN FOR A LIFETIME: HOW WOMEN INVESTORS
CAN GET THEIR GROOVE BACK

1. McKinsey and Company. (2011) "The Second Act Begins for ETFs." White paper.

2. Soe, Aye M., CFA. (Mid-year 2013) "S&P Indices Versus Active Funds (SPIVA) Scorecard." McGraw Hill Financial, pp. 1–27, http://www.spindices.com/documents/spiva/spiva-us-mid-year-2013.pdf

12 FIVE CRITICAL LESSONS AND WARNINGS: DON'T TOUCH A HOT STOVE, DON'T TALK TO STRANGERS, AND OTHER LESSONS FOR THE AGES

1. Amenta, Michael, CFA. (December 2013) FACTSET Dividend Quarterly, pp. 1–14.
2. Arnott, Robert D., and Asness, Clifford S. (January–February2003) "Surprise! Higher Dividends = Higher Earnings Growth." Financial Analysts Journal, 70–87.

14 IF YOU ARE GOING TO HIRE A PROFESSIONAL INVESTMENT ADVISOR, LET'S MAKE SURE YOU HIRE THE BEST: YOU REALLY CAN DO THIS ON YOUR OWN BUT FOR THOSE OF YOU WHO WON'T, CONSIDER THE FOLLOWING GUIDELINES

1. Silverstein, Michael J., Kato, Kosuke, and Tischhauser, Pia. (October 2009) "Women Want More (in Financial Services)." The Boston Consulting Group, www.bcg.perspectives.com
2. Longo, Tracey. (August 2001) "The Emerging Profile of Women Investors." Financial Advisor.

INDEX